Appointment Planner & Business organizer

IT IS GOING TO BE A GREAT WEEK!

If Found Please Contact:

_____

_____

_____

_____

SUPPLIES:	MONDAY DATE____/____/_____
	TUESDAY DATE____/____/_____
	WEDNESDAY DATE____/____/_____

THURSDAY DATE____/____/_____

CALLS

FRIDAY DATE___/___/____

SATURDAY DATE___/___/____

SUNDAY DATE___/___/____

SUPPLIES:	MONDAY	DATE____/____/_____
	TUESDAY	DATE____/____/_____
	WEDNESDAY	DATE____/____/_____

THURSDAY	DATE___/___/_____	CALLS

FRIDAY	DATE___/___/_____	

SATURDAY DATE___/___/____	SUNDAY DATE___/___/____

SUPPLIES:

MONDAY   DATE____/____/_____

TUESDAY   DATE____/____/_____

WEDNESDAY   DATE____/____/_____

THURSDAY	DATE___/___/_____	CALLS

FRIDAY	DATE___/___/____	

SATURDAY DATE___/___/____	SUNDAY DATE___/___/____

SUPPLIES:	MONDAY DATE____/____/_____
	TUESDAY DATE____/____/_____
	WEDNESDAY DATE____/____/_____

THURSDAY	DATE___/___/_____	CALLS

FRIDAY	DATE___/___/_____

SATURDAY DATE___/___/_____	SUNDAY DATE___/___/_____

SUPPLIES:	MONDAY	DATE____/____/_____
	TUESDAY	DATE____/____/_____
	WEDNESDAY	DATE____/____/_____

THURSDAY	DATE___/___/_____	CALLS

FRIDAY DATE___/___/____

SATURDAY DATE___/___/____ | **SUNDAY** DATE___/___/____

SUPPLIES:	MONDAY	DATE____/____/_____
	TUESDAY	DATE____/____/_____
	WEDNESDAY	DATE____/____/_____

THURSDAY	DATE___/___/_____	CALLS

FRIDAY	DATE___/___/____	

SATURDAY	DATE___/___/____	SUNDAY	DATE___/___/____

SUPPLIES:	MONDAY DATE____/____/_____
	TUESDAY DATE____/___/_____
	WEDNESDAY DATE____/____/_____

THURSDAY	DATE___/___/_____	CALLS

FRIDAY	DATE___/___/____	

SATURDAY DATE___/___/____	SUNDAY DATE___/___/____

SUPPLIES:	MONDAY	DATE____/____/_____
	TUESDAY	DATE____/____/_____
	WEDNESDAY	DATE____/____/_____

THURSDAY   DATE____/____/_____

CALLS

FRIDAY   DATE___/___/____

SATURDAY   DATE___/___/____

SUNDAY   DATE___/___/____

SUPPLIES:	MONDAY	DATE____/____/_____
	TUESDAY	DATE____/____/_____
	WEDNESDAY	DATE____/____/_____

THURSDAY	DATE____/____/_____	CALLS

FRIDAY	DATE___/___/____	

SATURDAY DATE___/___/____	SUNDAY DATE___/___/____

SUPPLIES:	MONDAY	DATE____/____/_____
	TUESDAY	DATE____/____/_____
	WEDNESDAY	DATE____/____/_____

THURSDAY	DATE___/___/_____	CALLS

FRIDAY	DATE___/___/____	

SATURDAY DATE___/___/____	SUNDAY DATE___/___/____

SUPPLIES:	MONDAY	DATE____/____/_____
	TUESDAY	DATE____/___/_____
	WEDNESDAY	DATE____/____/_____

THURSDAY   DATE____/____/_____

CALLS

FRIDAY   DATE___/___/____

SATURDAY   DATE___/___/____   **SUNDAY**   DATE___/___/____

SUPPLIES:	MONDAY	DATE____/____/_____
	TUESDAY	DATE____/____/_____
	WEDNESDAY	DATE____/____/_____

THURSDAY	DATE___/___/_____	CALLS

FRIDAY	DATE___/___/____	

SATURDAY DATE___/___/____	SUNDAY DATE___/___/____

SUPPLIES:	MONDAY DATE____/____/_____
	TUESDAY DATE____/____/_____
	WEDNESDAY DATE____/____/_____

THURSDAY	DATE___/___/_____	CALLS

FRIDAY DATE___/___/____

SATURDAY DATE___/___/____	SUNDAY DATE___/___/____

SUPPLIES:	MONDAY	DATE___/___/_____
	TUESDAY	DATE___/___/_____
	WEDNESDAY	DATE___/___/_____

THURSDAY	DATE___/___/_____	CALLS

FRIDAY	DATE___/___/_____

SATURDAY DATE___/___/_____	SUNDAY DATE___/___/_____

SUPPLIES:	MONDAY	DATE____/____/_____
	TUESDAY	DATE____/____/_____
	WEDNESDAY	DATE____/____/_____

THURSDAY	DATE___/___/_____	CALLS

FRIDAY	DATE___/___/____	

SATURDAY DATE___/___/____	SUNDAY DATE___/___/____

SUPPLIES:

MONDAY   DATE____/____/_____

TUESDAY   DATE____/____/_____

WEDNESDAY   DATE____/____/_____

THURSDAY	DATE___/___/_____	CALLS

FRIDAY	DATE___/___/____	

SATURDAY DATE___/___/____	SUNDAY DATE___/___/____

SUPPLIES:	MONDAY	DATE____/____/_____
	TUESDAY	DATE____/____/_____
	WEDNESDAY	DATE____/____/_____

THURSDAY	DATE___/___/_____	CALLS

FRIDAY	DATE___/___/____

SATURDAY DATE___/___/____	SUNDAY DATE___/___/____

SUPPLIES:	MONDAY	DATE____/____/_____
	TUESDAY	DATE____/____/_____
	WEDNESDAY	DATE____/____/_____

THURSDAY	DATE___/___/_____	CALLS

FRIDAY	DATE___/___/_____	

SATURDAY DATE___/___/_____	SUNDAY DATE___/___/_____

SUPPLIES:	MONDAY	DATE____/____/_____

TUESDAY   DATE____/____/_____

WEDNESDAY   DATE____/____/_____

THURSDAY	DATE___/___/_____	CALLS

FRIDAY	DATE___/___/____

SATURDAY DATE___/___/____	SUNDAY DATE___/___/____

SUPPLIES:	MONDAY	DATE___/___/_____
	TUESDAY	DATE___/___/_____
	WEDNESDAY	DATE___/___/_____

THURSDAY	DATE____/____/_____	CALLS

FRIDAY	DATE___/___/____

SATURDAY DATE___/___/____	SUNDAY DATE___/___/____

SUPPLIES:	MONDAY	DATE____/____/_____
	TUESDAY	DATE____/____/_____
	WEDNESDAY	DATE____/____/_____

THURSDAY	DATE___/___/_____	CALLS

FRIDAY	DATE___/___/____	

SATURDAY DATE___/___/____	SUNDAY DATE___/___/____

SUPPLIES:	MONDAY	DATE____/____/_____
	TUESDAY	DATE____/____/_____
	WEDNESDAY	DATE____/____/_____

THURSDAY	DATE____/____/_____	CALLS

FRIDAY   DATE___/___/____

SATURDAY DATE___/___/____	SUNDAY DATE___/___/____

SUPPLIES:	MONDAY	DATE____/____/_____
	TUESDAY	DATE____/____/_____
	WEDNESDAY	DATE____/____/_____

THURSDAY	DATE___/___/_____	CALLS

FRIDAY	DATE___/___/____

SATURDAY	DATE___/___/____	SUNDAY	DATE___/___/____

SUPPLIES:	MONDAY	DATE___/___/_____
	TUESDAY	DATE___/___/_____
	WEDNESDAY	DATE___/___/_____

THURSDAY	DATE___/___/_____	CALLS

FRIDAY	DATE___/___/_____

SATURDAY DATE___/___/____	SUNDAY DATE___/___/____

SUPPLIES:

MONDAY   DATE____/____/_____

TUESDAY   DATE____/____/_____

WEDNESDAY   DATE____/____/_____

THURSDAY	DATE___/___/_____	CALLS

FRIDAY	DATE___/___/____	

SATURDAY	DATE___/___/____	SUNDAY	DATE___/___/____

SUPPLIES:	MONDAY	DATE____/____/_____
	TUESDAY	DATE____/____/_____
	WEDNESDAY	DATE____/____/_____

THURSDAY   DATE____/____/_____

CALLS

FRIDAY   DATE___/___/____

SATURDAY   DATE___/___/____

SUNDAY   DATE___/___/____

SUPPLIES:	MONDAY	DATE____/____/_____
	TUESDAY	DATE____/____/_____
	WEDNESDAY	DATE____/____/_____

THURSDAY	DATE___/___/_____	CALLS

FRIDAY	DATE___/___/____	

SATURDAY DATE___/___/____	SUNDAY DATE___/___/____

SUPPLIES:	MONDAY DATE____/____/_____
	TUESDAY DATE____/____/_____
	WEDNESDAY DATE____/____/_____

THURSDAY   DATE____/____/_____

CALLS

FRIDAY   DATE___/___/____

SATURDAY   DATE___/___/____

SUNDAY   DATE___/___/____

SUPPLIES:	MONDAY	DATE____/____/_____
	TUESDAY	DATE____/____/_____
	WEDNESDAY	DATE____/____/_____

THURSDAY   DATE____/____/_____

CALLS

FRIDAY   DATE___/___/____

SATURDAY   DATE___/___/____   **SUNDAY**   DATE___/___/____

SUPPLIES:	MONDAY	DATE___/___/_____
	TUESDAY	DATE___/___/_____
	WEDNESDAY	DATE___/___/_____

THURSDAY	DATE___/___/_____	CALLS

FRIDAY	DATE___/___/____	

SATURDAY DATE___/___/____	SUNDAY DATE___/___/____

SUPPLIES:	MONDAY DATE____/____/_____
	TUESDAY DATE____/___/_____
	WEDNESDAY DATE____/____/_____

THURSDAY   DATE____/____/_____

CALLS

FRIDAY   DATE___/___/____

SATURDAY   DATE___/___/____   **SUNDAY**   DATE___/___/____

SUPPLIES:	MONDAY	DATE____/____/_____
	TUESDAY	DATE____/____/_____
	WEDNESDAY	DATE____/____/_____

THURSDAY   DATE_____/_____/_____

CALLS

FRIDAY   DATE____/____/_____

SATURDAY   DATE___/___/____

SUNDAY   DATE___/___/____

SUPPLIES:	MONDAY	DATE____/____/_____
	TUESDAY	DATE____/____/_____
	WEDNESDAY	DATE____/____/_____

THURSDAY	DATE___/___/_____	CALLS

FRIDAY	DATE___/___/____	

SATURDAY DATE___/___/____	SUNDAY DATE___/___/____

SUPPLIES:	MONDAY	DATE___/___/_____
	TUESDAY	DATE___/___/_____
	WEDNESDAY	DATE___/___/_____

THURSDAY   DATE____/____/_____   **CALLS**

FRIDAY   DATE___/___/____

SATURDAY   DATE___/___/____   **SUNDAY**   DATE___/___/____

SUPPLIES:	MONDAY	DATE____/____/_____
	TUESDAY	DATE____/____/_____
	WEDNESDAY	DATE____/____/_____

THURSDAY	DATE___/___/_____	CALLS

FRIDAY	DATE___/___/____	

SATURDAY DATE___/___/____	SUNDAY DATE___/___/____

SUPPLIES:	MONDAY	DATE____/____/_____
	TUESDAY	DATE____/____/_____
	WEDNESDAY	DATE____/____/_____

THURSDAY	DATE___/___/_____	CALLS

FRIDAY	DATE__/__/____	

SATURDAY DATE__/__/____	SUNDAY DATE__/__/____

SUPPLIES:	MONDAY	DATE____/____/_____
	TUESDAY	DATE____/____/_____
	WEDNESDAY	DATE____/____/_____

THURSDAY	DATE____/____/_____	CALLS

FRIDAY	DATE___/___/____

SATURDAY DATE___/___/____	SUNDAY DATE___/___/____

SUPPLIES:	MONDAY	DATE___/___/_____

TUESDAY DATE___/___/_____

WEDNESDAY DATE___/___/_____

THURSDAY	DATE___/___/_____	CALLS

FRIDAY	DATE___/___/____

SATURDAY DATE___/___/____	SUNDAY DATE___/___/____

SUPPLIES:	MONDAY	DATE____/____/_____
	TUESDAY	DATE____/____/_____
	WEDNESDAY	DATE____/____/_____

THURSDAY	DATE___/___/_____	CALLS

FRIDAY DATE___/___/____

SATURDAY DATE___/___/____	SUNDAY DATE___/___/____

SUPPLIES:	MONDAY	DATE____/____/_____
	TUESDAY	DATE____/____/_____
	WEDNESDAY	DATE____/____/_____

THURSDAY	DATE___/___/_____	CALLS

FRIDAY	DATE___/___/____

SATURDAY DATE___/___/____	SUNDAY DATE___/___/____

SUPPLIES:	MONDAY	DATE____/____/_____
	TUESDAY	DATE____/____/_____
	WEDNESDAY	DATE____/____/_____

THURSDAY	DATE____/____/_____	CALLS

FRIDAY	DATE___/___/____	

SATURDAY DATE___/___/____	SUNDAY DATE___/___/____

SUPPLIES:	MONDAY	DATE____/____/_____
	TUESDAY	DATE____/____/_____
	WEDNESDAY	DATE____/____/_____

THURSDAY	DATE___/___/_____	CALLS

FRIDAY	DATE___/___/____	

SATURDAY DATE___/___/____	SUNDAY DATE___/___/____

SUPPLIES:	MONDAY	DATE____/____/_____
	TUESDAY	DATE____/____/_____
	WEDNESDAY	DATE____/____/_____

THURSDAY	DATE___/___/_____	CALLS

FRIDAY	DATE___/___/____	

SATURDAY DATE___/___/____	SUNDAY DATE___/___/____

SUPPLIES:	MONDAY	DATE____/____/_____
	TUESDAY	DATE____/____/_____
	WEDNESDAY	DATE____/____/_____

THURSDAY	DATE____/____/_____	CALLS

FRIDAY   DATE___/___/____

CALLS

SATURDAY DATE___/___/____	SUNDAY DATE___/___/____

SUPPLIES:	MONDAY	DATE____/____/_____
	TUESDAY	DATE____/____/_____
	WEDNESDAY	DATE____/____/_____

THURSDAY	DATE___/___/_____	CALLS

FRIDAY	DATE___/___/____	

SATURDAY DATE___/___/____	SUNDAY DATE___/___/____

SUPPLIES:	MONDAY DATE___/___/_____
	TUESDAY DATE___/___/_____
	WEDNESDAY DATE___/___/_____

THURSDAY   DATE____/____/_____

CALLS

FRIDAY   DATE___/___/____

SATURDAY   DATE___/___/____

SUNDAY   DATE___/___/____

SUPPLIES:	MONDAY	DATE____/____/_____
	TUESDAY	**DATE____/____/_____**
	WEDNESDAY	**DATE____/____/_____**

THURSDAY	DATE___/___/_____	CALLS

FRIDAY	DATE___/___/____	CALLS

SATURDAY DATE___/___/____	SUNDAY DATE___/___/____

SUPPLIES:	MONDAY	DATE___/___/_____
	TUESDAY	DATE___/___/_____
	WEDNESDAY	DATE___/___/_____

THURSDAY   DATE____/____/_____

CALLS

FRIDAY   DATE___/___/____

SATURDAY   DATE___/___/____

SUNDAY   DATE___/___/____

SUPPLIES:	MONDAY DATE____/____/_____
	TUESDAY DATE____/____/_____
	WEDNESDAY DATE____/____/_____

THURSDAY   DATE____/____/_____

CALLS

FRIDAY   DATE___/___/____

SATURDAY   DATE___/___/____

SUNDAY   DATE___/___/____

SUPPLIES:	MONDAY	DATE____/____/_____
	TUESDAY	DATE____/____/_____
	WEDNESDAY	DATE____/____/_____

THURSDAY	DATE___/___/_____	CALLS

FRIDAY	DATE___/___/____	

SATURDAY DATE___/___/____	SUNDAY DATE___/___/____

SUPPLIES:	MONDAY	DATE____/____/_____
	TUESDAY	DATE____/____/_____
	WEDNESDAY	DATE____/____/_____

THURSDAY	DATE___/___/_____	CALLS

FRIDAY	DATE___/___/____	

SATURDAY DATE___/___/____	SUNDAY DATE___/___/____

SUPPLIES:	MONDAY	DATE____/____/_____
	TUESDAY	DATE____/____/_____
	WEDNESDAY	DATE____/____/_____

THURSDAY	DATE___/___/_____	CALLS

FRIDAY	DATE___/___/____

SATURDAY	DATE___/___/____	SUNDAY	DATE___/___/____

2024

January
M	T	W	T	F	S	S
1	2	3	4	5	6	7
8	9	10	11	12	13	14
15	16	17	18	19	20	21
22	23	24	25	26	27	28
29	30	31				

February
M	T	W	T	F	S	S
			1	2	3	4
5	6	7	8	9	10	11
12	13	14	15	16	17	18
19	20	21	22	23	24	25
26	27	28	29			

March
M	T	W	T	F	S	S
				1	2	3
4	5	6	7	8	9	10
11	12	13	14	15	16	17
18	19	20	21	22	23	24
25	26	27	28	29	30	31

April
M	T	W	T	F	S	S
1	2	3	4	5	6	7
8	9	10	11	12	13	14
15	16	17	18	19	20	21
22	23	24	25	26	27	28
29	30					

May
M	T	W	T	F	S	S
		1	2	3	4	5
6	7	8	9	10	11	12
13	14	15	16	17	18	19
20	21	22	23	24	25	26
27	28	29	30	31		

June
M	T	W	T	F	S	S
					1	2
3	4	5	6	7	8	9
10	11	12	13	14	15	16
17	18	19	20	21	22	23
24	25	26	27	28	29	30

July
M	T	W	T	F	S	S
1	2	3	4	5	6	7
8	9	10	11	12	13	14
15	16	17	18	19	20	21
22	23	24	25	26	27	28
29	30	31				

August
M	T	W	T	F	S	S
			1	2	3	4
5	6	7	8	9	10	11
12	13	14	15	16	17	18
19	20	21	22	23	24	25
26	27	28	29	30	31	

September
M	T	W	T	F	S	S
						1
2	3	4	5	6	7	8
9	10	11	12	13	14	15
16	17	18	19	20	21	22
23	24	25	26	27	28	29
30						

October
M	T	W	T	F	S	S
	1	2	3	4	5	6
7	8	9	10	11	12	13
14	15	16	17	18	19	20
21	22	23	24	25	26	27
28	29	30	31			

November
M	T	W	T	F	S	S
				1	2	3
4	5	6	7	8	9	10
11	12	13	14	15	16	17
18	19	20	21	22	23	24
25	26	27	28	29	30	

December
M	T	W	T	F	S	S
						1
2	3	4	5	6	7	8
9	10	11	12	13	14	15
16	17	18	19	20	21	22
23	24	25	26	27	28	29
30	31					

2025

January
M	T	W	T	F	S	S
		1	2	3	4	5
6	7	8	9	10	11	12
13	14	15	16	17	18	19
20	21	22	23	24	25	26
27	28	29	30	31		

February
M	T	W	T	F	S	S
					1	2
3	4	5	6	7	8	9
10	11	12	13	14	15	16
17	18	19	20	21	22	23
24	25	26	27	28		

March
M	T	W	T	F	S	S
					1	2
3	4	5	6	7	8	9
10	11	12	13	14	15	16
17	18	19	20	21	22	23
24	25	26	27	28	29	30
31						

April
M	T	W	T	F	S	S
	1	2	3	4	5	6
7	8	9	10	11	12	13
14	15	16	17	18	19	20
21	22	23	24	25	26	27
28	29	30				

May
M	T	W	T	F	S	S
			1	2	3	4
5	6	7	8	9	10	11
12	13	14	15	16	17	18
19	20	21	22	23	24	25
26	27	28	29	30	31	

June
M	T	W	T	F	S	S
						1
2	3	4	5	6	7	8
9	10	11	12	13	14	15
16	17	18	19	20	21	22
23	24	25	26	27	28	29
30						

July
M	T	W	T	F	S	S
	1	2	3	4	5	6
7	8	9	10	11	12	13
14	15	16	17	18	19	20
21	22	23	24	25	26	27
28	29	30	31			

August
M	T	W	T	F	S	S
				1	2	3
4	5	6	7	8	9	10
11	12	13	14	15	16	17
18	19	20	21	22	23	24
25	26	27	28	29	30	31

September
M	T	W	T	F	S	S
1	2	3	4	5	6	7
8	9	10	11	12	13	14
15	16	17	18	19	20	21
22	23	24	25	26	27	28
29	30					

October
M	T	W	T	F	S	S
		1	2	3	4	5
6	7	8	9	10	11	12
13	14	15	16	17	18	19
20	21	22	23	24	25	26
27	28	29	30	31		

November
M	T	W	T	F	S	S
					1	2
3	4	5	6	7	8	9
10	11	12	13	14	15	16
17	18	19	20	21	22	23
24	25	26	27	28	29	30

December
M	T	W	T	F	S	S
1	2	3	4	5	6	7
8	9	10	11	12	13	14
15	16	17	18	19	20	21
22	23	24	25	26	27	28
29	30	31				

2026

January

M	T	W	T	F	S	S
			1	2	3	4
5	6	7	8	9	10	11
12	13	14	15	16	17	18
19	20	21	22	23	24	25
26	27	28	29	30	31	

February

M	T	W	T	F	S	S
						1
2	3	4	5	6	7	8
9	10	11	12	13	14	15
16	17	18	19	20	21	22
23	24	25	26	27	28	

March

M	T	W	T	F	S	S
						1
2	3	4	5	6	7	8
9	10	11	12	13	14	15
16	17	18	19	20	21	22
23	24	25	26	27	28	29
30	31					

April

M	T	W	T	F	S	S
	1	2	3	4	5
6	7	8	9	10	11	12
13	14	15	16	17	18	19
20	21	22	23	24	25	26
27	28	29	30			

May

M	T	W	T	F	S	S
				1	2	3
4	5	6	7	8	9	10
11	12	13	14	15	16	17
18	19	20	21	22	23	24
25	26	27	28	29	30	31

June

M	T	W	T	F	S	S
1	2	3	4	5	6	7
8	9	10	11	12	13	14
15	16	17	18	19	20	21
22	23	24	25	26	27	28
29	30					

July

M	T	W	T	F	S	S
		1	2	3	4	5
6	7	8	9	10	11	12
13	14	15	16	17	18	19
20	21	22	23	24	25	26
27	28	29	30	31		

August

M	T	W	T	F	S	S
					1	2
3	4	5	6	7	8	9
10	11	12	13	14	15	16
17	18	19	20	21	22	23
24	25	26	27	28	29	30
31						

September

M	T	W	T	F	S	S
1	2	3	4	5	6
7	8	9	10	11	12	13
14	15	16	17	18	19	20
21	22	23	24	25	26	27
28	29	30				

October

M	T	W	T	F	S	S
			1	2	3	4
5	6	7	8	9	10	11
12	13	14	15	16	17	18
19	20	21	22	23	24	25
26	27	28	29	30	31	

November

M	T	W	T	F	S	S
						1
2	3	4	5	6	7	8
9	10	11	12	13	14	15
16	17	18	19	20	21	22
23	24	25	26	27	28	29
30						

December

M	T	W	T	F	S	S
1	2	3	4	5	6
7	8	9	10	11	12	13
14	15	16	17	18	19	20
21	22	23	24	25	26	27
28	29	30	31			

2027

January
M	T	W	T	F	S	S
				1	2	3
4	5	6	7	8	9	10
11	12	13	14	15	16	17
18	19	20	21	22	23	24
25	26	27	28	29	30	31

February
M	T	W	T	F	S	S
1	2	3	4	5	6	7
8	9	10	11	12	13	14
15	16	17	18	19	20	21
22	23	24	25	26	27	28

March
M	T	W	T	F	S	S
1	2	3	4	5	6	7
8	9	10	11	12	13	14
15	16	17	18	19	20	21
22	23	24	25	26	27	28
29	30	31				

April
M	T	W	T	F	S	S
			1	2	3	4
5	6	7	8	9	10	11
12	13	14	15	16	17	18
19	20	21	22	23	24	25
26	27	28	29	30		

May
M	T	W	T	F	S	S
					1	2
3	4	5	6	7	8	9
10	11	12	13	14	15	16
17	18	19	20	21	22	23
24	25	26	27	28	29	30
31						

June
M	T	W	T	F	S	S
	1	2	3	4	5	6
7	8	9	10	11	12	13
14	15	16	17	18	19	20
21	22	23	24	25	26	27
28	29	30				

July
M	T	W	T	F	S	S
			1	2	3	4
5	6	7	8	9	10	11
12	13	14	15	16	17	18
19	20	21	22	23	24	25
26	27	28	29	30	31	

August
M	T	W	T	F	S	S
						1
2	3	4	5	6	7	8
9	10	11	12	13	14	15
16	17	18	19	20	21	22
23	24	25	26	27	28	29
30	31					

September
M	T	W	T	F	S	S
		1	2	3	4	5
6	7	8	9	10	11	12
13	14	15	16	17	18	19
20	21	22	23	24	25	26
27	28	29	30			

October
M	T	W	T	F	S	S
				1	2	3
4	5	6	7	8	9	10
11	12	13	14	15	16	17
18	19	20	21	22	23	24
25	26	27	28	29	30	31

November
M	T	W	T	F	S	S
1	2	3	4	5	6	7
8	9	10	11	12	13	14
15	16	17	18	19	20	21
22	23	24	25	26	27	28
29	30					

December
M	T	W	T	F	S	S
		1	2	3	4	5
6	7	8	9	10	11	12
13	14	15	16	17	18	19
20	21	22	23	24	25	26
27	28	29	30	31		

2028

January

M	T	W	T	F	S	S
					1	2
3	4	5	6	7	8	9
10	11	12	13	14	15	16
17	18	19	20	21	22	23
24	25	26	27	28	29	30
31						

February

M	T	W	T	F	S	S
	1	2	3	4	5	6
7	8	9	10	11	12	13
14	15	16	17	18	19	20
21	22	23	24	25	26	27
28	29					

March

M	T	W	T	F	S	S
		1	2	3	4	5
6	7	8	9	10	11	12
13	14	15	16	17	18	19
20	21	22	23	24	25	26
27	28	29	30	31		

April

M	T	W	T	F	S	S
					1	2
3	4	5	6	7	8	9
10	11	12	13	14	15	16
17	18	19	20	21	22	23
24	25	26	27	28	29	30

May

M	T	W	T	F	S	S
1	2	3	4	5	6	7
8	9	10	11	12	13	14
15	16	17	18	19	20	21
22	23	24	25	26	27	28
29	30	31				

June

M	T	W	T	F	S	S
			1	2	3	4
5	6	7	8	9	10	11
12	13	14	15	16	17	18
19	20	21	22	23	24	25
26	27	28	29	30		

July

M	T	W	T	F	S	S
					1	2
3	4	5	6	7	8	9
10	11	12	13	14	15	16
17	18	19	20	21	22	23
24	25	26	27	28	29	30
31						

August

M	T	W	T	F	S	S
	1	2	3	4	5	6
7	8	9	10	11	12	13
14	15	16	17	18	19	20
21	22	23	24	25	26	27
28	29	30	31			

September

M	T	W	T	F	S	S
				1	2	3
4	5	6	7	8	9	10
11	12	13	14	15	16	17
18	19	20	21	22	23	24
25	26	27	28	29	30	

October

M	T	W	T	F	S	S
						1
2	3	4	5	6	7	8
9	10	11	12	13	14	15
16	17	18	19	20	21	22
23	24	25	26	27	28	29
30	31					

November

M	T	W	T	F	S	S
		1	2	3	4	5
6	7	8	9	10	11	12
13	14	15	16	17	18	19
20	21	22	23	24	25	26
27	28	29	30			

December

M	T	W	T	F	S	S
				1	2	3
4	5	6	7	8	9	10
11	12	13	14	15	16	17
18	19	20	21	22	23	24
25	26	27	28	29	30	31

2029

January
M	T	W	T	F	S	S
1	2	3	4	5	6	7
8	9	10	11	12	13	14
15	16	17	18	19	20	21
22	23	24	25	26	27	28
29	30	31				

February
M	T	W	T	F	S	S
			1	2	3	4
5	6	7	8	9	10	11
12	13	14	15	16	17	18
19	20	21	22	23	24	25
26	27	28				

March
M	T	W	T	F	S	S
			1	2	3	4
5	6	7	8	9	10	11
12	13	14	15	16	17	18
19	20	21	22	23	24	25
26	27	28	29	30	31	

April
M	T	W	T	F	S	S
						1
2	3	4	5	6	7	8
9	10	11	12	13	14	15
16	17	18	19	20	21	22
23	24	25	26	27	28	29
30						

May
M	T	W	T	F	S	S
	1	2	3	4	5	6
7	8	9	10	11	12	13
14	15	16	17	18	19	20
21	22	23	24	25	26	27
28	29	30	31			

June
M	T	W	T	F	S	S
				1	2	3
4	5	6	7	8	9	10
11	12	13	14	15	16	17
18	19	20	21	22	23	24
25	26	27	28	29	30	

July
M	T	W	T	F	S	S
						1
2	3	4	5	6	7	8
9	10	11	12	13	14	15
16	17	18	19	20	21	22
23	24	25	26	27	28	29
30	31					

August
M	T	W	T	F	S	S
		1	2	3	4	5
6	7	8	9	10	11	12
13	14	15	16	17	18	19
20	21	22	23	24	25	26
27	28	29	30	31		

September
M	T	W	T	F	S	S
					1	2
3	4	5	6	7	8	9
10	11	12	13	14	15	16
17	18	19	20	21	22	23
24	25	26	27	28	29	30

October
M	T	W	T	F	S	S
1	2	3	4	5	6	7
8	9	10	11	12	13	14
15	16	17	18	19	20	21
22	23	24	25	26	27	28
29	30	31				

November
M	T	W	T	F	S	S
			1	2	3	4
5	6	7	8	9	10	11
12	13	14	15	16	17	18
19	20	21	22	23	24	25
26	27	28	29	30		

December
M	T	W	T	F	S	S
					1	2
3	4	5	6	7	8	9
10	11	12	13	14	15	16
17	18	19	20	21	22	23
24	25	26	27	28	29	30
31						

2030

January

M	T	W	T	F	S	S
	1	2	3	4	5	6
7	8	9	10	11	12	13
14	15	16	17	18	19	20
21	22	23	24	25	26	27
28	29	30	31			

February

M	T	W	T	F	S	S
				1	2	3
4	5	6	7	8	9	10
11	12	13	14	15	16	17
18	19	20	21	22	23	24
25	26	27	28			

March

M	T	W	T	F	S	S
				1	2	3
4	5	6	7	8	9	10
11	12	13	14	15	16	17
18	19	20	21	22	23	24
25	26	27	28	29	30	31

April

M	T	W	T	F	S	S
1	2	3	4	5	6	7
8	9	10	11	12	13	14
15	16	17	18	19	20	21
22	23	24	25	26	27	28
29	30					

May

M	T	W	T	F	S	S
		1	2	3	4	5
6	7	8	9	10	11	12
13	14	15	16	17	18	19
20	21	22	23	24	25	26
27	28	29	30	31		

June

M	T	W	T	F	S	S
					1	2
3	4	5	6	7	8	9
10	11	12	13	14	15	16
17	18	19	20	21	22	23
24	25	26	27	28	29	30

July

M	T	W	T	F	S	S
1	2	3	4	5	6	7
8	9	10	11	12	13	14
15	16	17	18	19	20	21
22	23	24	25	26	27	28
29	30	31				

August

M	T	W	T	F	S	S
			1	2	3	4
5	6	7	8	9	10	11
12	13	14	15	16	17	18
19	20	21	22	23	24	25
26	27	28	29	30	31	

September

M	T	W	T	F	S	S
						1
2	3	4	5	6	7	8
9	10	11	12	13	14	15
16	17	18	19	20	21	22
23	24	25	26	27	28	29
30						

October

M	T	W	T	F	S	S
	1	2	3	4	5	6
7	8	9	10	11	12	13
14	15	16	17	18	19	20
21	22	23	24	25	26	27
28	29	30	31			

November

M	T	W	T	F	S	S
				1	2	3
4	5	6	7	8	9	10
11	12	13	14	15	16	17
18	19	20	21	22	23	24
25	26	27	28	29	30	

December

M	T	W	T	F	S	S
						1
2	3	4	5	6	7	8
9	10	11	12	13	14	15
16	17	18	19	20	21	22
23	24	25	26	27	28	29
30	31					

2031

January
M	T	W	T	F	S	S
	1	2	3	4	5
6	7	8	9	10	11	12
13	14	15	16	17	18	19
20	21	22	23	24	25	26
27	28	29	30	31		

February
M	T	W	T	F	S	S
					1	2
3	4	5	6	7	8	9
10	11	12	13	14	15	16
17	18	19	20	21	22	23
24	25	26	27	28		

March
M	T	W	T	F	S	S
					1	2
3	4	5	6	7	8	9
10	11	12	13	14	15	16
17	18	19	20	21	22	23
24	25	26	27	28	29	30
31						

April
M	T	W	T	F	S	S
	1	2	3	4	5	6
7	8	9	10	11	12	13
14	15	16	17	18	19	20
21	22	23	24	25	26	27
28	29	30				

May
M	T	W	T	F	S	S
			1	2	3	4
5	6	7	8	9	10	11
12	13	14	15	16	17	18
19	20	21	22	23	24	25
26	27	28	29	30	31	

June
M	T	W	T	F	S	S
						1
2	3	4	5	6	7	8
9	10	11	12	13	14	15
16	17	18	19	20	21	22
23	24	25	26	27	28	29
30						

July
M	T	W	T	F	S	S
	1	2	3	4	5	6
7	8	9	10	11	12	13
14	15	16	17	18	19	20
21	22	23	24	25	26	27
28	29	30	31			

August
M	T	W	T	F	S	S
				1	2	3
4	5	6	7	8	9	10
11	12	13	14	15	16	17
18	19	20	21	22	23	24
25	26	27	28	29	30	31

September
M	T	W	T	F	S	S
1	2	3	4	5	6	7
8	9	10	11	12	13	14
15	16	17	18	19	20	21
22	23	24	25	26	27	28
29	30					

October
M	T	W	T	F	S	S
	1	2	3	4	5
6	7	8	9	10	11	12
13	14	15	16	17	18	19
20	21	22	23	24	25	26
27	28	29	30	31		

November
M	T	W	T	F	S	S
					1	2
3	4	5	6	7	8	9
10	11	12	13	14	15	16
17	18	19	20	21	22	23
24	25	26	27	28	29	30

December
M	T	W	T	F	S	S
1	2	3	4	5	6	7
8	9	10	11	12	13	14
15	16	17	18	19	20	21
22	23	24	25	26	27	28
29	30	31				

2032

January

M	T	W	T	F	S	S
			1	2	3	4
5	6	7	8	9	10	11
12	13	14	15	16	17	18
19	20	21	22	23	24	25
26	27	28	29	30	31	

February

M	T	W	T	F	S	S
						1
2	3	4	5	6	7	8
9	10	11	12	13	14	15
16	17	18	19	20	21	22
23	24	25	26	27	28	29

March

M	T	W	T	F	S	S
1	2	3	4	5	6	7
8	9	10	11	12	13	14
15	16	17	18	19	20	21
22	23	24	25	26	27	28
29	30	31				

April

M	T	W	T	F	S	S
			1	2	3	4
5	6	7	8	9	10	11
12	13	14	15	16	17	18
19	20	21	22	23	24	25
26	27	28	29	30		

May

M	T	W	T	F	S	S
					1	2
3	4	5	6	7	8	9
10	11	12	13	14	15	16
17	18	19	20	21	22	23
24	25	26	27	28	29	30
31						

June

M	T	W	T	F	S	S
	1	2	3	4	5	6
7	8	9	10	11	12	13
14	15	16	17	18	19	20
21	22	23	24	25	26	27
28	29	30				

July

M	T	W	T	F	S	S
			1	2	3	4
5	6	7	8	9	10	11
12	13	14	15	16	17	18
19	20	21	22	23	24	25
26	27	28	29	30	31	

August

M	T	W	T	F	S	S
						1
2	3	4	5	6	7	8
9	10	11	12	13	14	15
16	17	18	19	20	21	22
23	24	25	26	27	28	29
30	31					

September

M	T	W	T	F	S	S
		1	2	3	4	5
6	7	8	9	10	11	12
13	14	15	16	17	18	19
20	21	22	23	24	25	26
27	28	29	30			

October

M	T	W	T	F	S	S
				1	2	3
4	5	6	7	8	9	10
11	12	13	14	15	16	17
18	19	20	21	22	23	24
25	26	27	28	29	30	31

November

M	T	W	T	F	S	S
1	2	3	4	5	6	7
8	9	10	11	12	13	14
15	16	17	18	19	20	21
22	23	24	25	26	27	28
29	30					

December

M	T	W	T	F	S	S
		1	2	3	4	5
6	7	8	9	10	11	12
13	14	15	16	17	18	19
20	21	22	23	24	25	26
27	28	29	30	31		

BUSINESS ASSOCIATE'S & CLIENT CONTACT INFORMATION

NAME	
PHONE #	
ADDRESS	
E-MAIL	
NOTES	

NAME	
PHONE #	
ADDRESS	
E-MAIL	
NOTES	

NAME	
PHONE #	
ADDRESS	
EMAIL	
NOTES	

B

NAME	
PHONE #	
ADDRESS	
E-MAIL	
NOTES	

NAME	
PHONE #	
ADDRESS	
E-MAIL	
NOTES	

NAME	
PHONE #	
ADDRESS	
EMAIL	
NOTES	

NAME	
PHONE #	
ADDRESS	
E-MAIL	
NOTES	

NAME	
PHONE #	
ADDRESS	
E-MAIL	
NOTES	

NAME	
PHONE #	
ADDRESS	
EMAIL	
NOTES	

D

NAME	
PHONE #	
ADDRESS	
E-MAIL	
NOTES	

NAME	
PHONE #	
ADDRESS	
E-MAIL	
NOTES	

NAME	
PHONE #	
ADDRESS	
EMAIL	
NOTES	

NAME	
PHONE #	
ADDRESS	
E-MAIL	
NOTES	

NAME	
PHONE #	
ADDRESS	
E-MAIL	
NOTES	

NAME	
PHONE #	
ADDRESS	
EMAIL	
NOTES	

F

NAME	
PHONE #	
ADDRESS	
E-MAIL	
NOTES	

NAME	
PHONE #	
ADDRESS	
E-MAIL	
NOTES	

NAME	
PHONE #	
ADDRESS	
EMAIL	
NOTES	

G

NAME	
PHONE #	
ADDRESS	
E-MAIL	
NOTES	

NAME	
PHONE #	
ADDRESS	
E-MAIL	
NOTES	

NAME	
PHONE #	
ADDRESS	
EMAIL	
NOTES	

H

NAME	
PHONE #	
ADDRESS	
E-MAIL	
NOTES	

NAME	
PHONE #	
ADDRESS	
E-MAIL	
NOTES	

NAME	
PHONE #	
ADDRESS	
EMAIL	
NOTES	

NAME	
PHONE #	
ADDRESS	
E-MAIL	
NOTES	

NAME	
PHONE #	
ADDRESS	
E-MAIL	
NOTES	

NAME	
PHONE #	
ADDRESS	
EMAIL	
NOTES	

J

NAME	
PHONE #	
ADDRESS	
E-MAIL	
NOTES	

NAME	
PHONE #	
ADDRESS	
E-MAIL	
NOTES	

NAME	
PHONE #	
ADDRESS	
EMAIL	
NOTES	

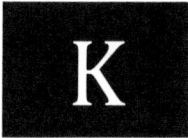

NAME	
PHONE #	
ADDRESS	
E-MAIL	
NOTES	

NAME	
PHONE #	
ADDRESS	
E-MAIL	
NOTES	

NAME	
PHONE #	
ADDRESS	
EMAIL	
NOTES	

L

NAME	
PHONE #	
ADDRESS	
E-MAIL	
NOTES	

NAME	
PHONE #	
ADDRESS	
E-MAIL	
NOTES	

NAME	
PHONE #	
ADDRESS	
EMAIL	
NOTES	

M

NAME	
PHONE #	
ADDRESS	
E-MAIL	
NOTES	

NAME	
PHONE #	
ADDRESS	
E-MAIL	
NOTES	

NAME	
PHONE #	
ADDRESS	
EMAIL	
NOTES	

N

NAME	
PHONE #	
ADDRESS	
E-MAIL	
NOTES	

NAME	
PHONE #	
ADDRESS	
E-MAIL	
NOTES	

NAME	
PHONE #	
ADDRESS	
EMAIL	
NOTES	

NAME	
PHONE #	
ADDRESS	
E-MAIL	
NOTES	

NAME	
PHONE #	
ADDRESS	
E-MAIL	
NOTES	

NAME	
PHONE #	
ADDRESS	
EMAIL	
NOTES	

P

NAME	
PHONE #	
ADDRESS	
E-MAIL	
NOTES	

NAME	
PHONE #	
ADDRESS	
E-MAIL	
NOTES	

NAME	
PHONE #	
ADDRESS	
EMAIL	
NOTES	

Q

NAME	
PHONE #	
ADDRESS	
E-MAIL	
NOTES	

NAME	
PHONE #	
ADDRESS	
E-MAIL	
NOTES	

NAME	
PHONE #	
ADDRESS	
EMAIL	
NOTES	

R

NAME	
PHONE #	
ADDRESS	
E-MAIL	
NOTES	

NAME	
PHONE #	
ADDRESS	
E-MAIL	
NOTES	

NAME	
PHONE #	
ADDRESS	
EMAIL	
NOTES	

NAME	
PHONE #	
ADDRESS	
E-MAIL	
NOTES	

NAME	
PHONE #	
ADDRESS	
E-MAIL	
NOTES	

NAME	
PHONE #	
ADDRESS	
EMAIL	
NOTES	

T

NAME	
PHONE #	
ADDRESS	
E-MAIL	
NOTES	

NAME	
PHONE #	
ADDRESS	
E-MAIL	
NOTES	

NAME	
PHONE #	
ADDRESS	
EMAIL	
NOTES	

U

NAME	
PHONE #	
ADDRESS	
E-MAIL	
NOTES	

NAME	
PHONE #	
ADDRESS	
E-MAIL	
NOTES	

NAME	
PHONE #	
ADDRESS	
EMAIL	
NOTES	

V

NAME	
PHONE #	
ADDRESS	
E-MAIL	
NOTES	

NAME	
PHONE #	
ADDRESS	
E-MAIL	
NOTES	

NAME	
PHONE #	
ADDRESS	
EMAIL	
NOTES	

W

NAME	
PHONE #	
ADDRESS	
E-MAIL	
NOTES	

NAME	
PHONE #	
ADDRESS	
E-MAIL	
NOTES	

NAME	
PHONE #	
ADDRESS	
EMAIL	
NOTES	

X

NAME	
PHONE #	
ADDRESS	
E-MAIL	
NOTES	

NAME	
PHONE #	
ADDRESS	
E-MAIL	
NOTES	

NAME	
PHONE #	
ADDRESS	
EMAIL	
NOTES	

Y

NAME	
PHONE #	
ADDRESS	
E-MAIL	
NOTES	

NAME	
PHONE #	
ADDRESS	
E-MAIL	
NOTES	

NAME	
PHONE #	
ADDRESS	
EMAIL	
NOTES	

Z

NAME	
PHONE #	
ADDRESS	
E-MAIL	
NOTES	

NAME	
PHONE #	
ADDRESS	
E-MAIL	
NOTES	

NAME	
PHONE #	
ADDRESS	
EMAIL	
NOTES	

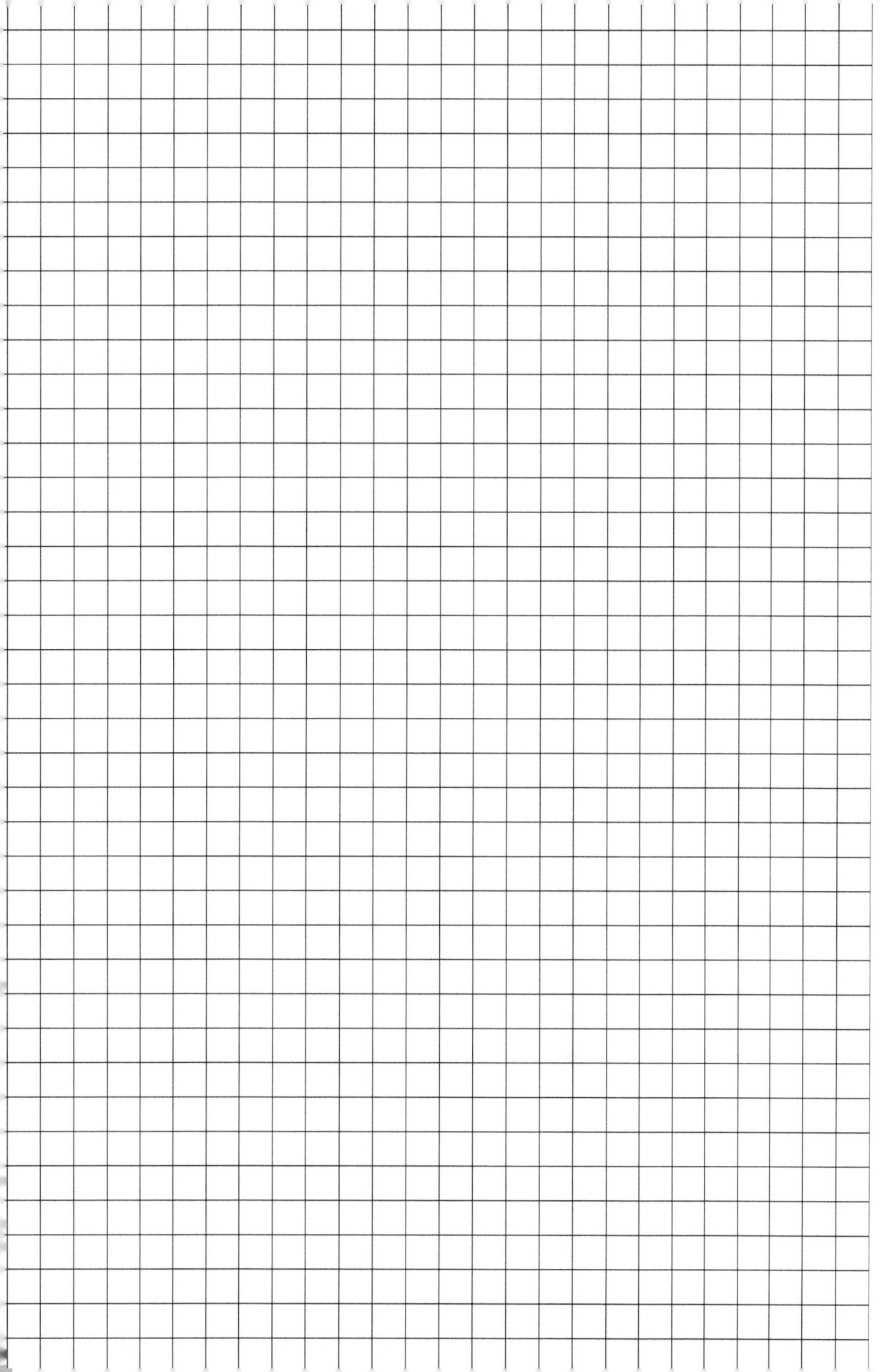

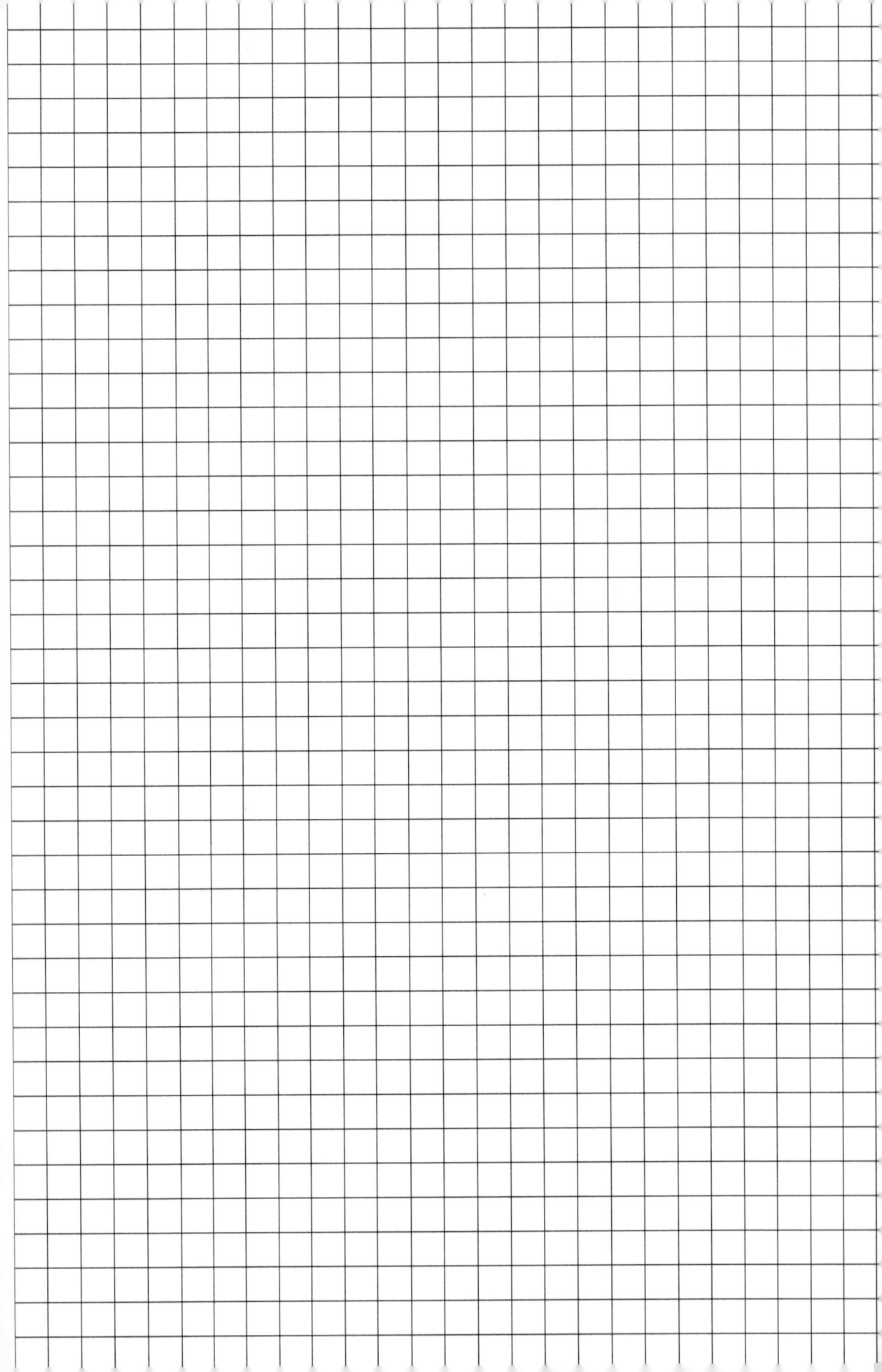

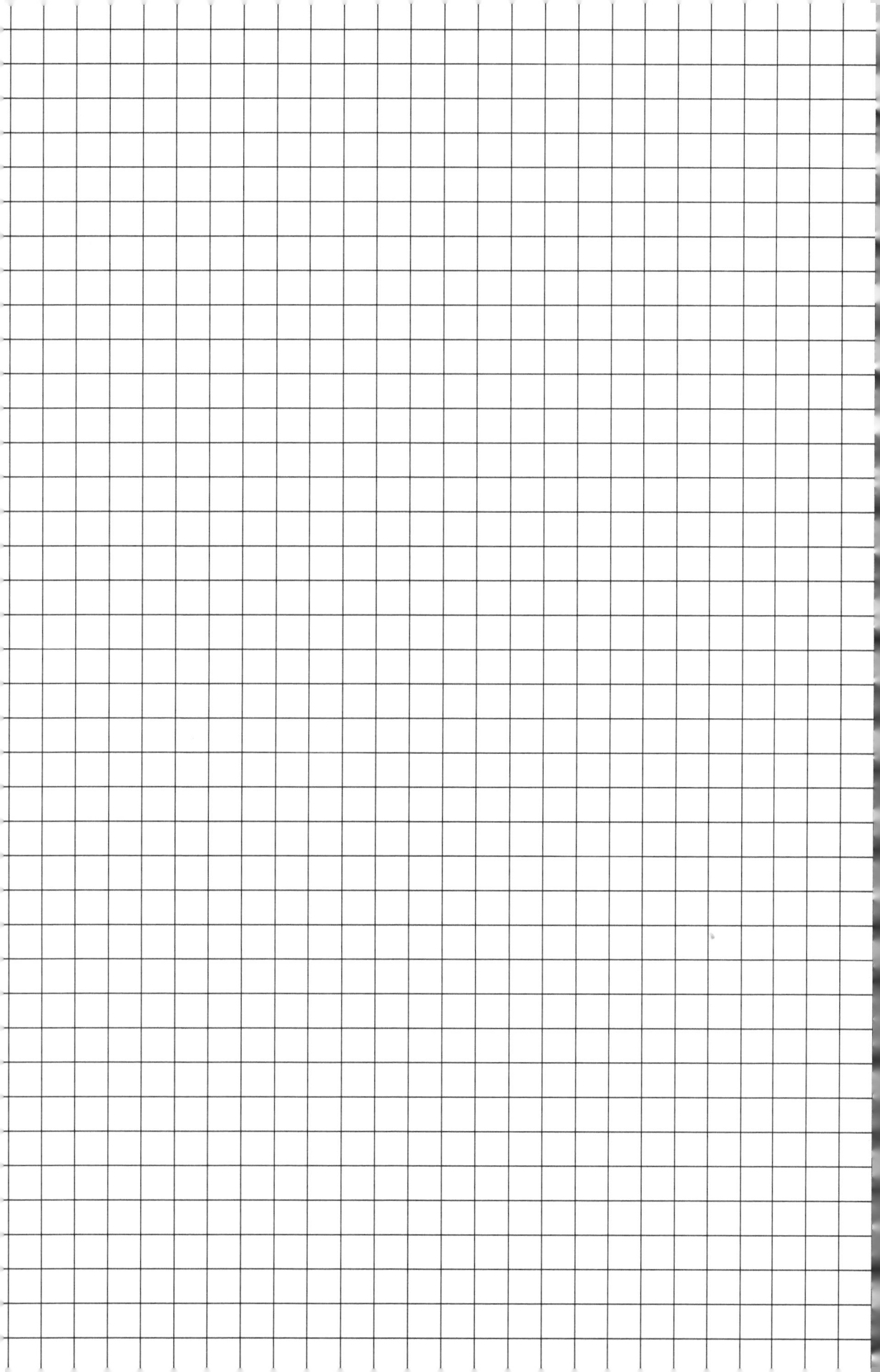

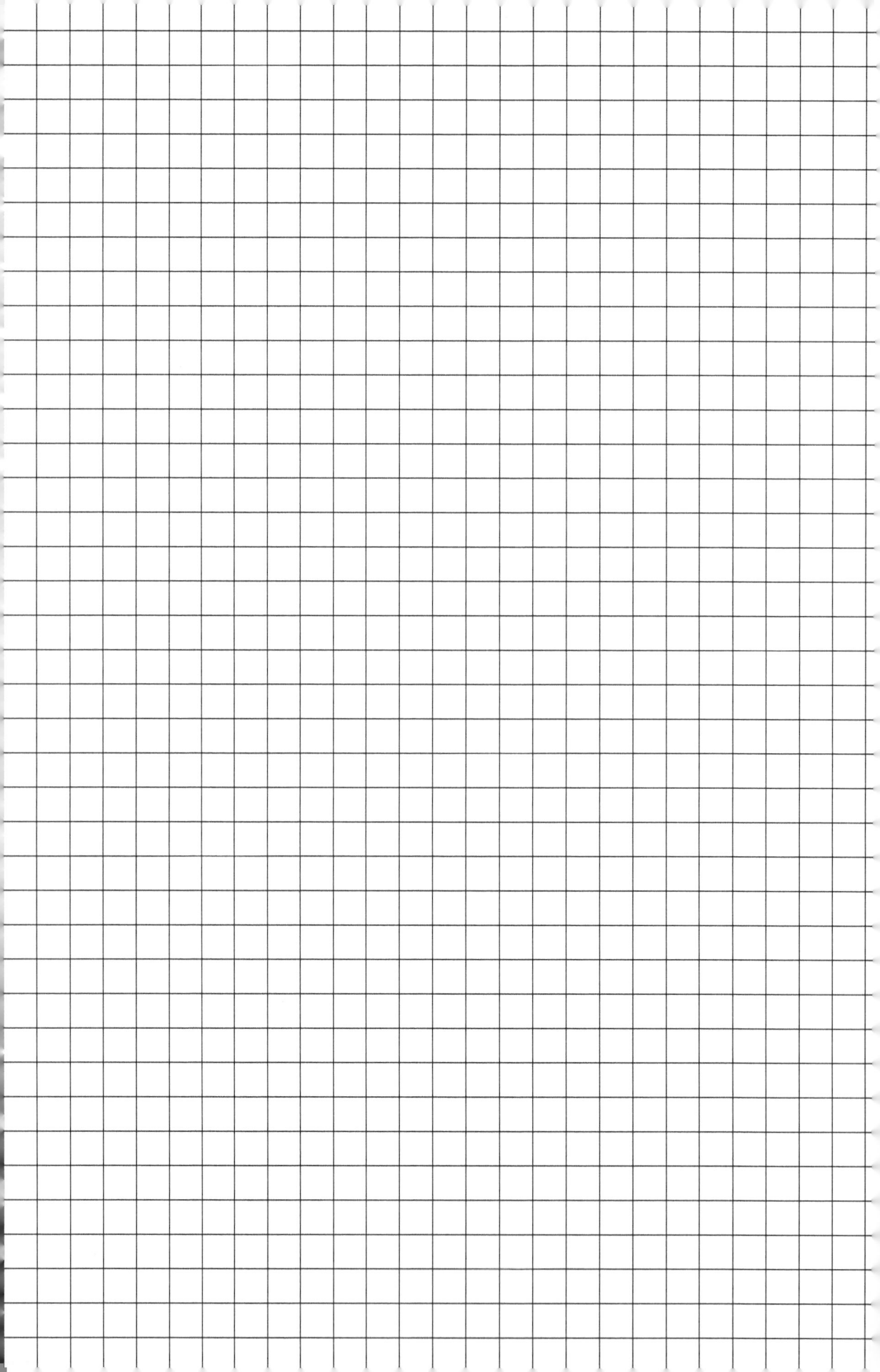

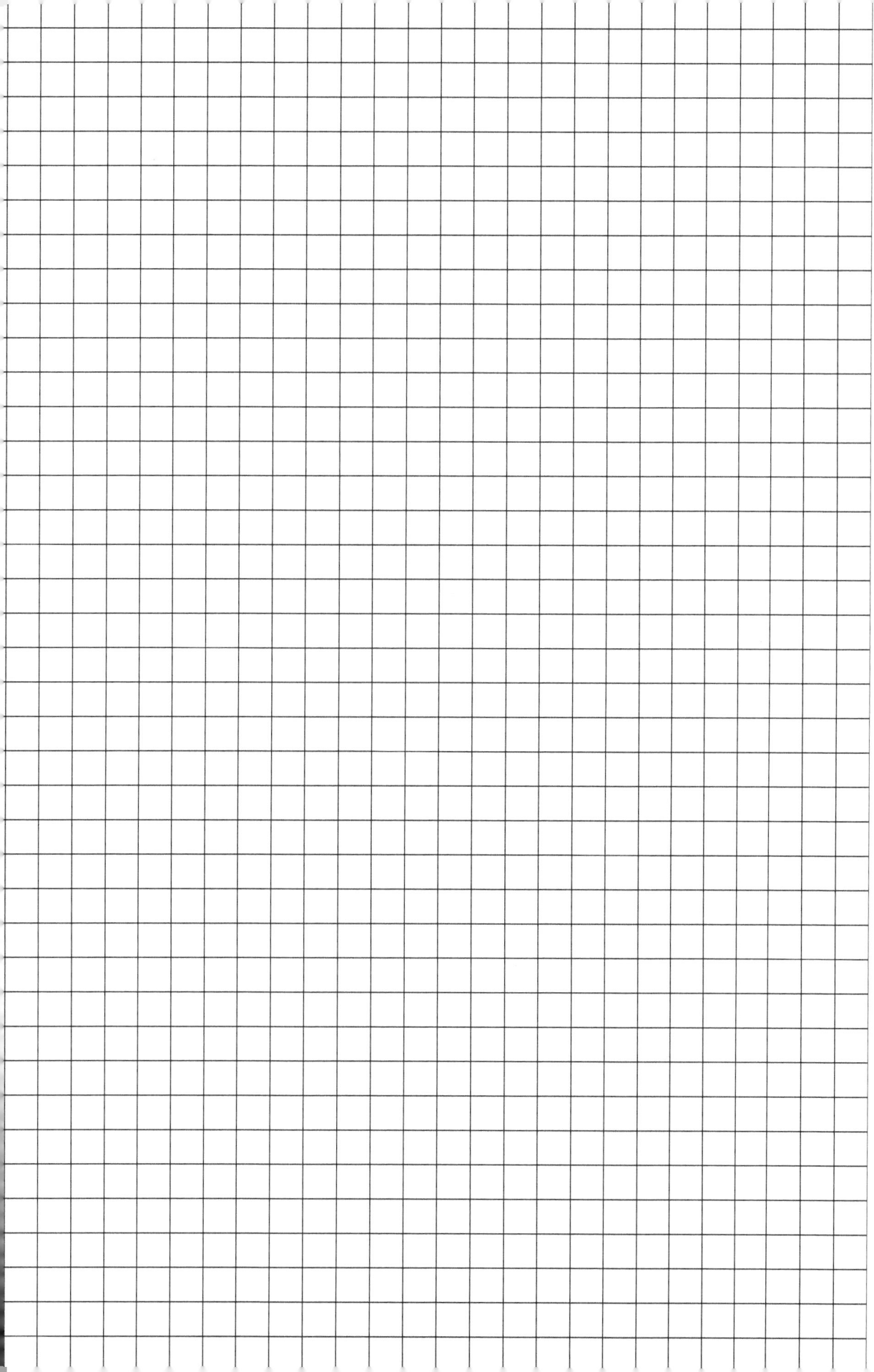

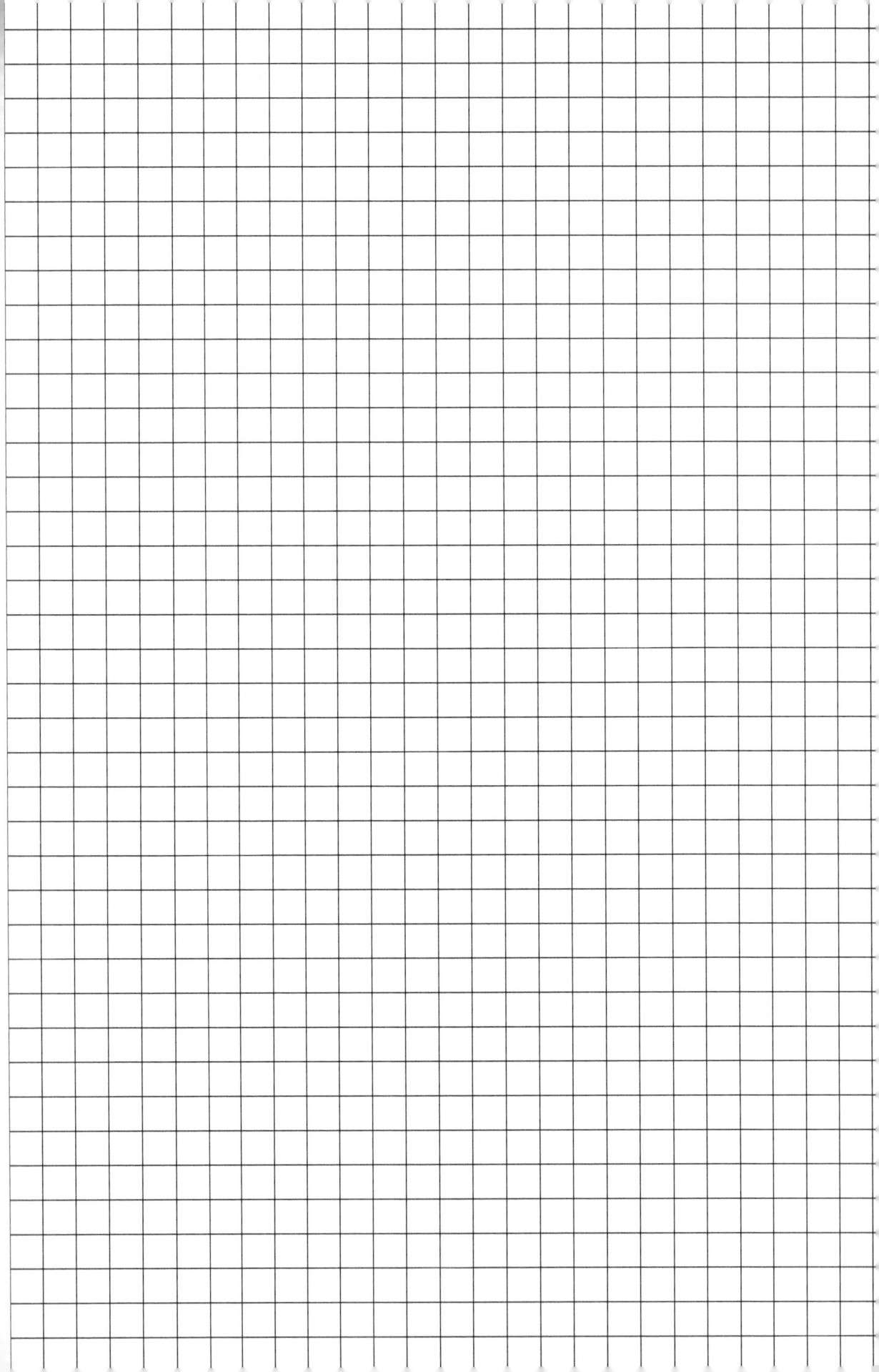

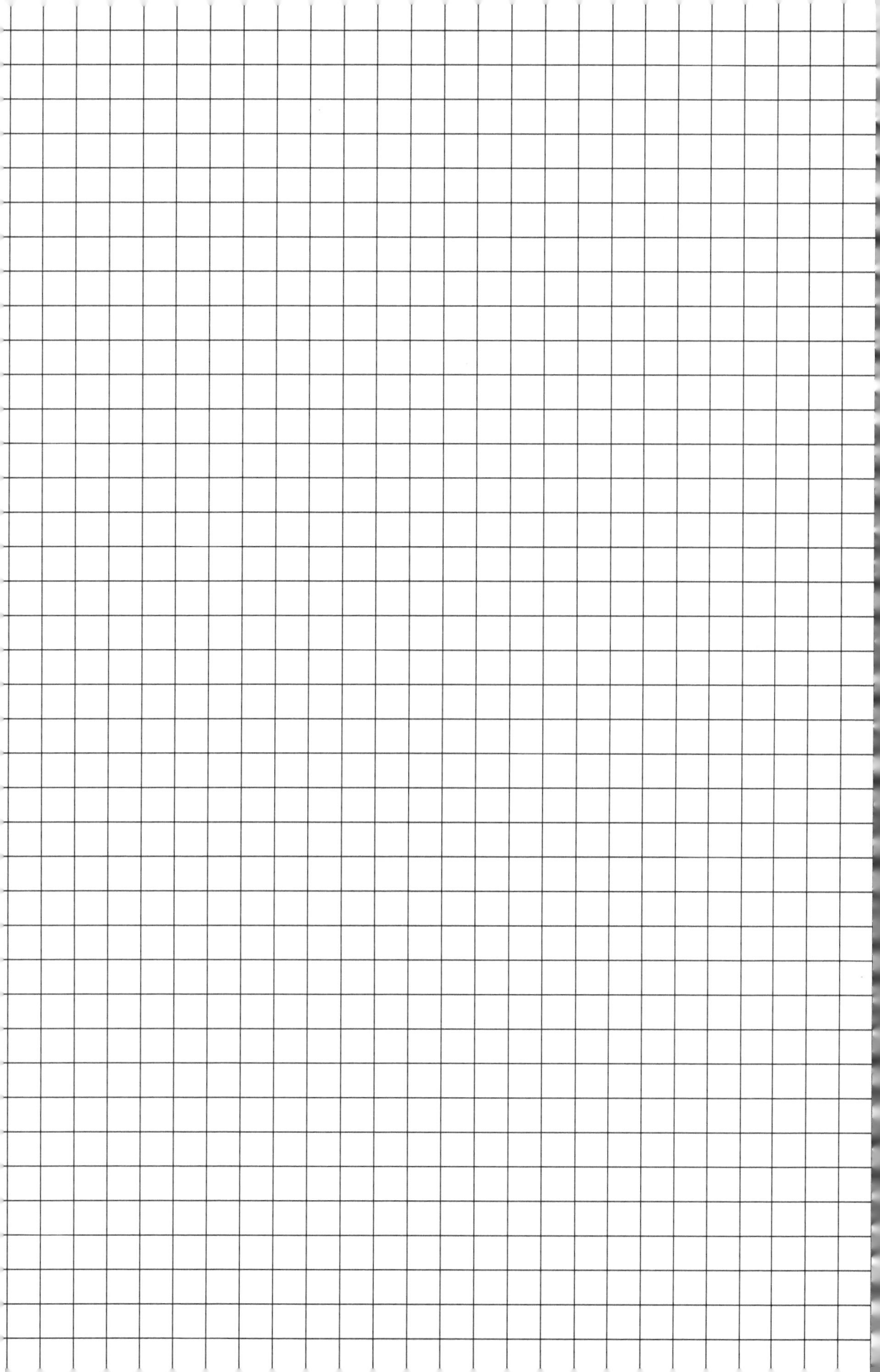

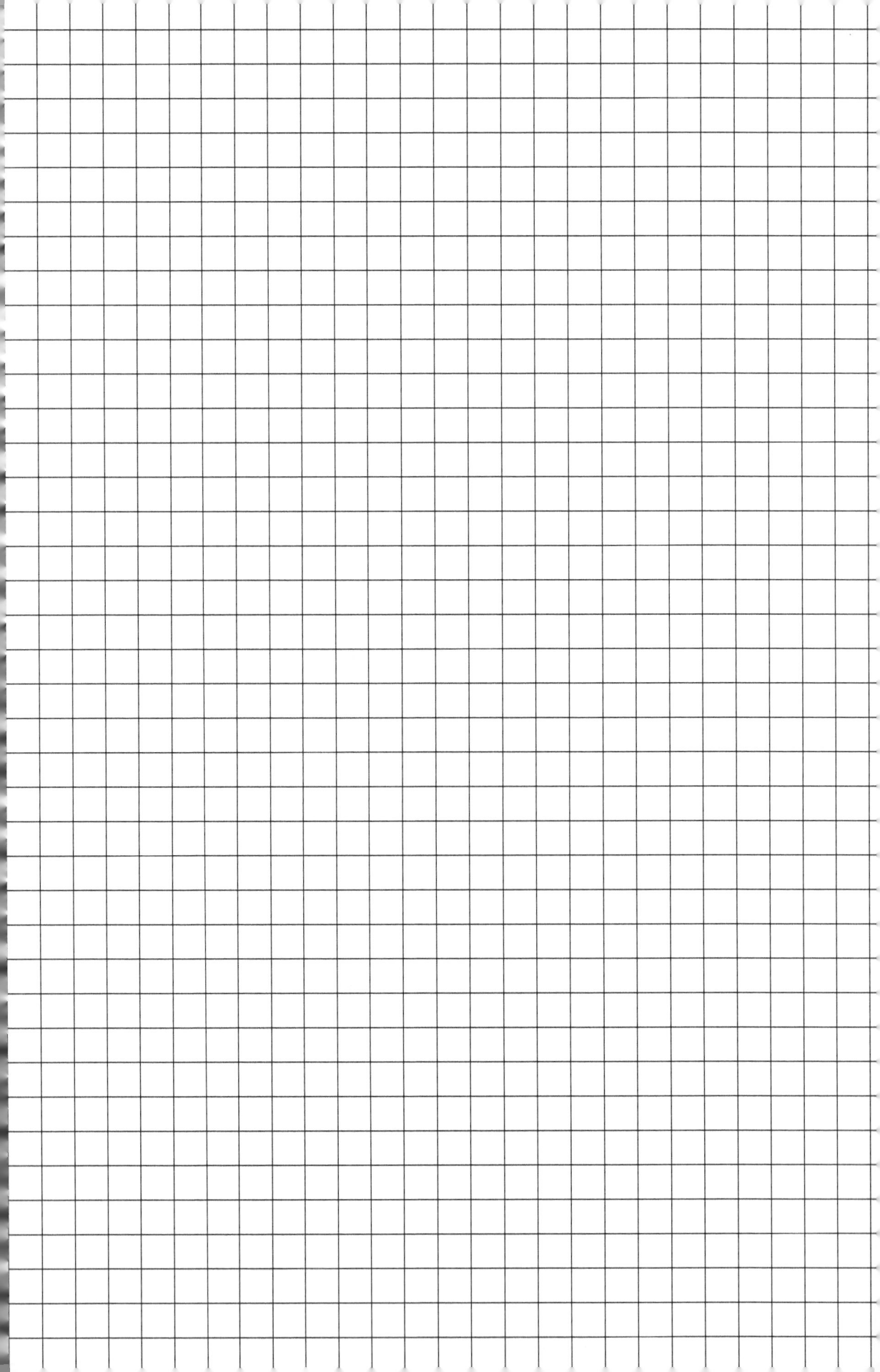

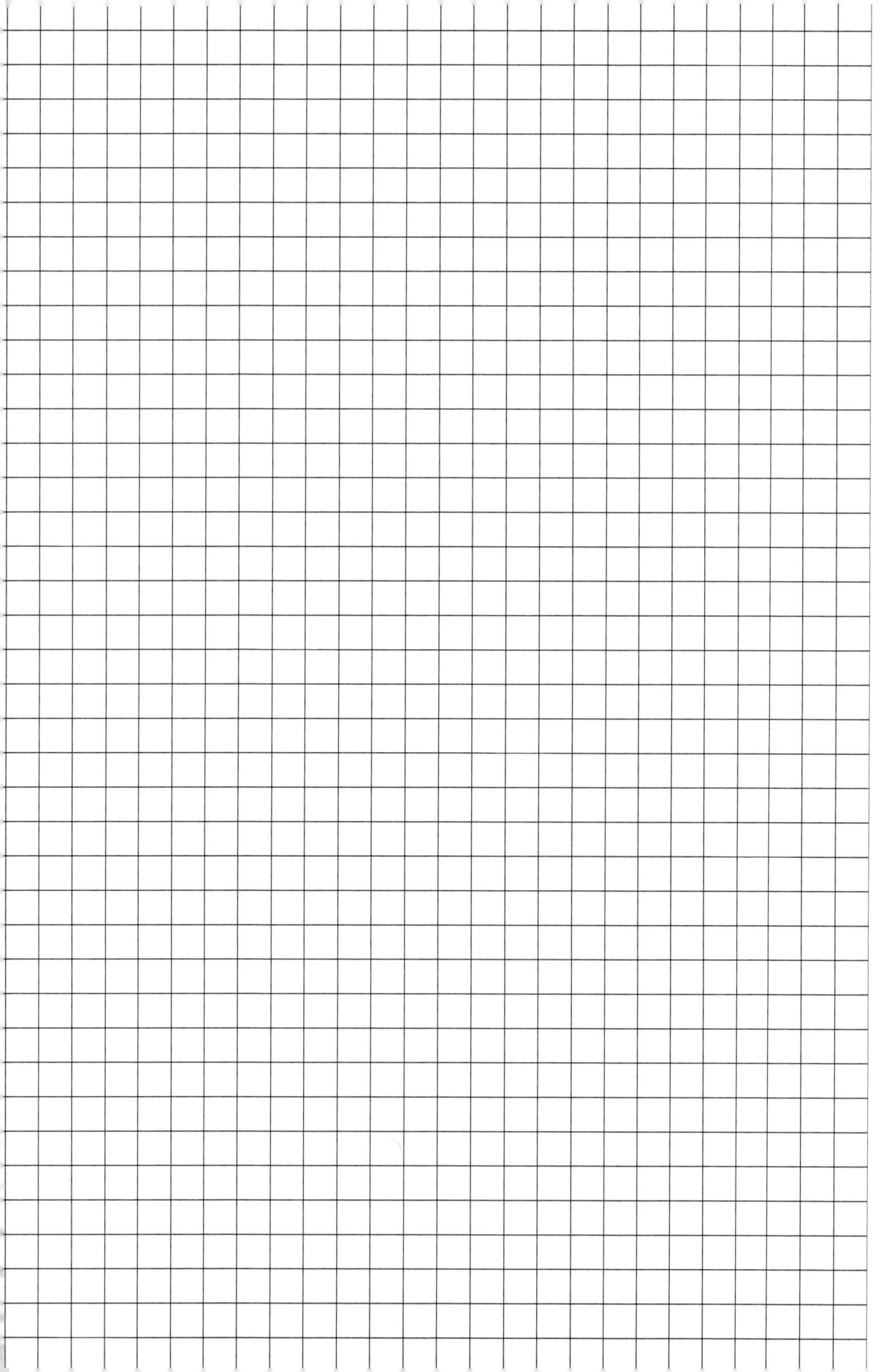

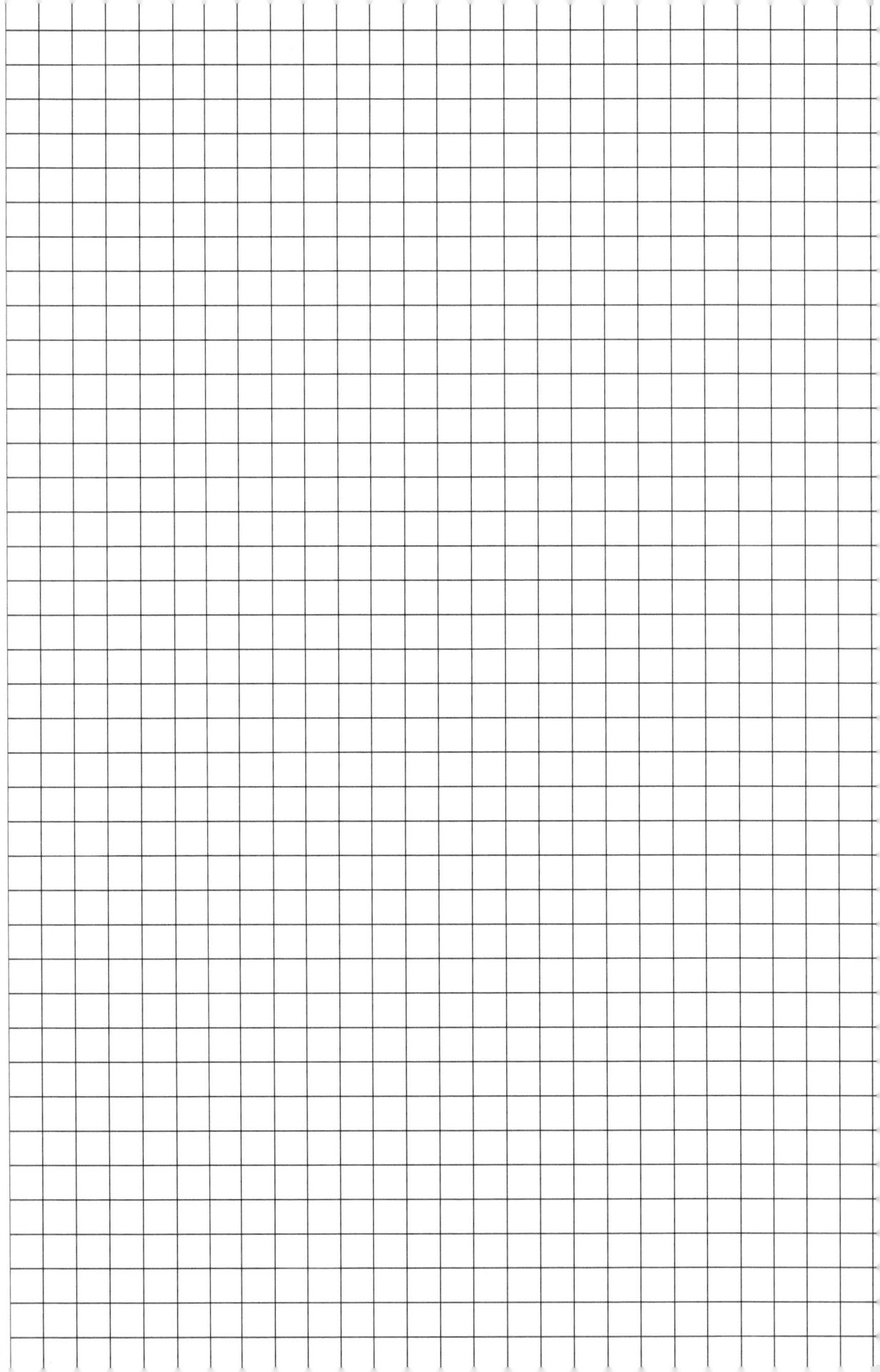

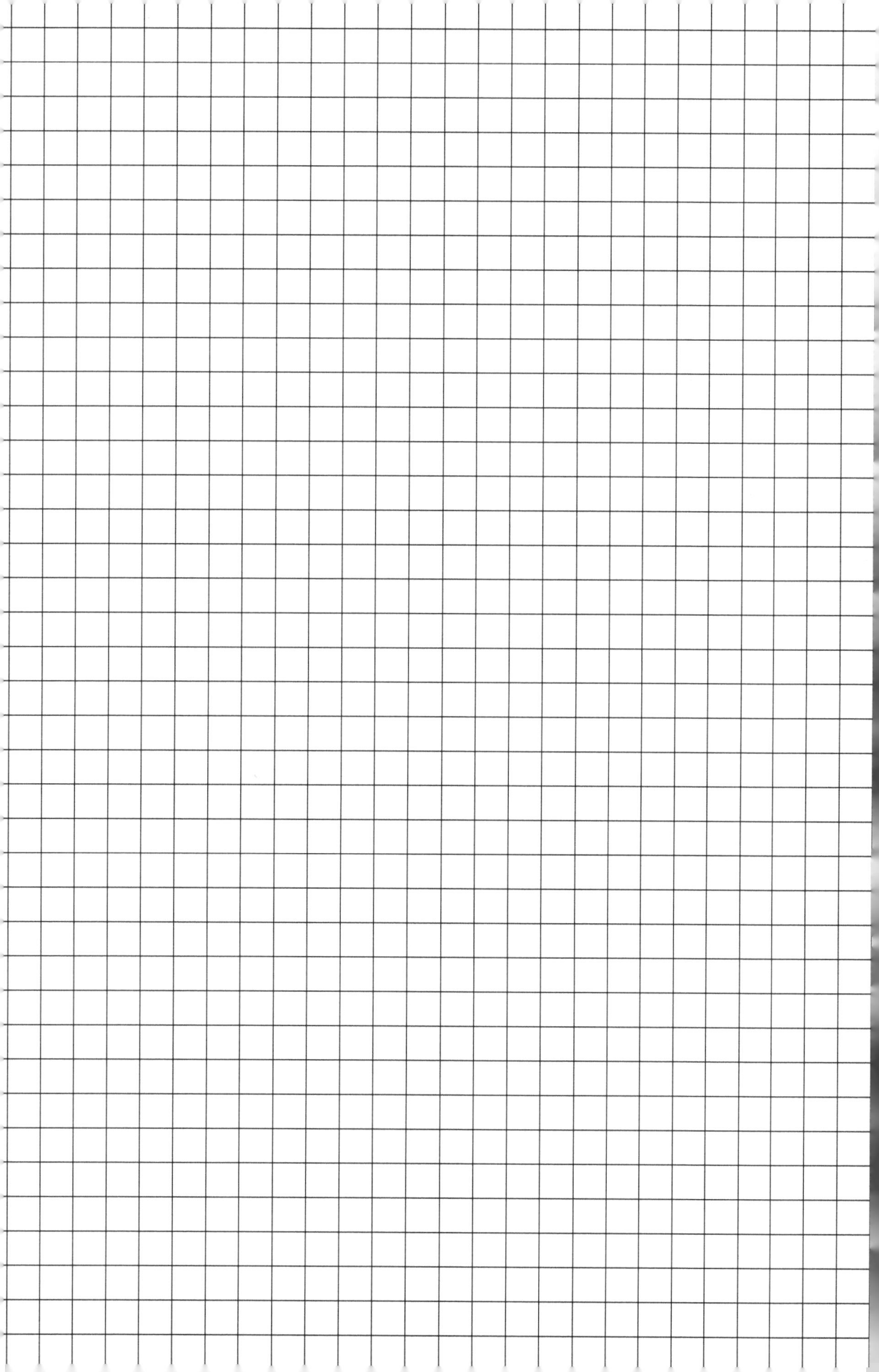

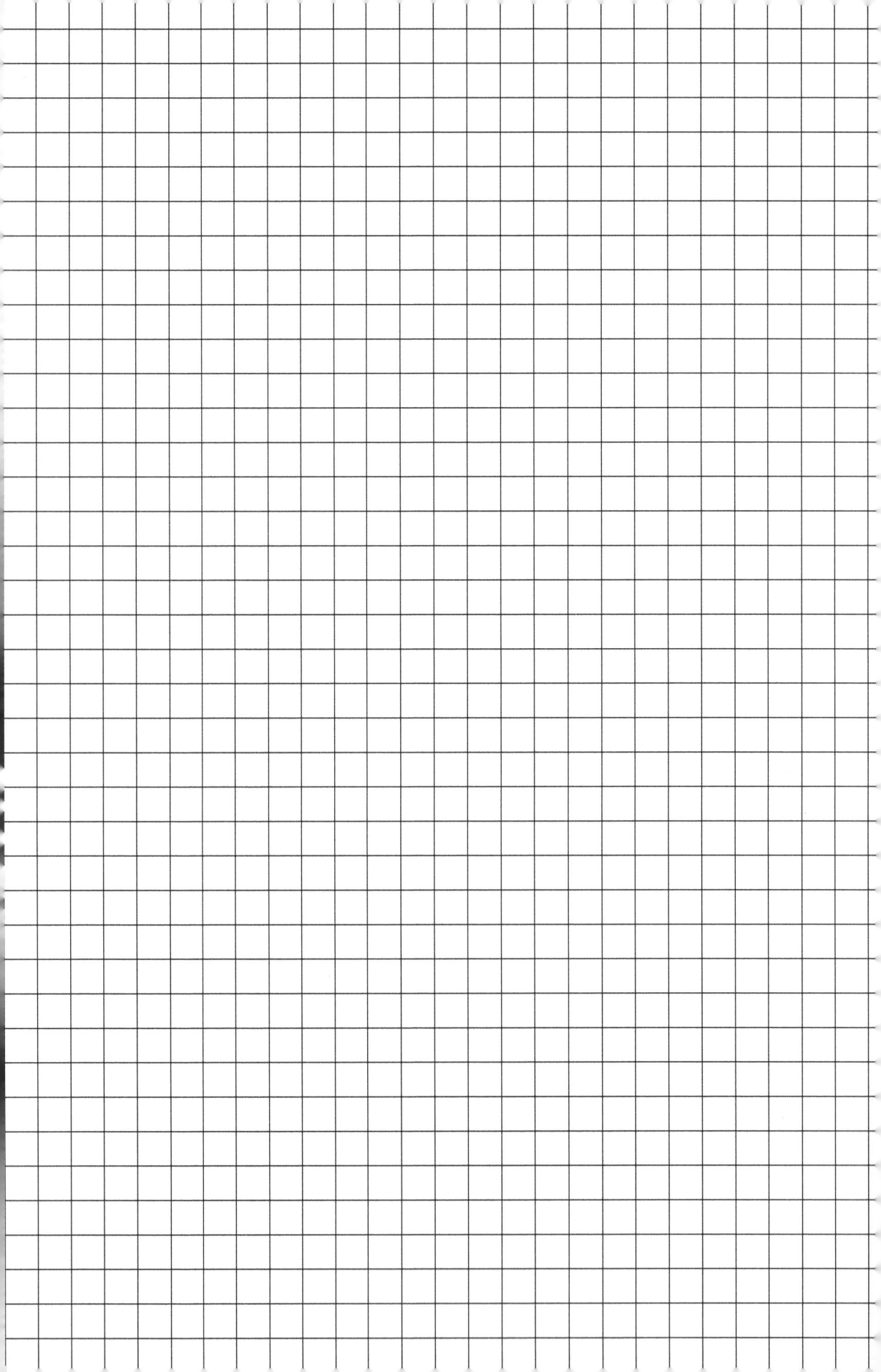

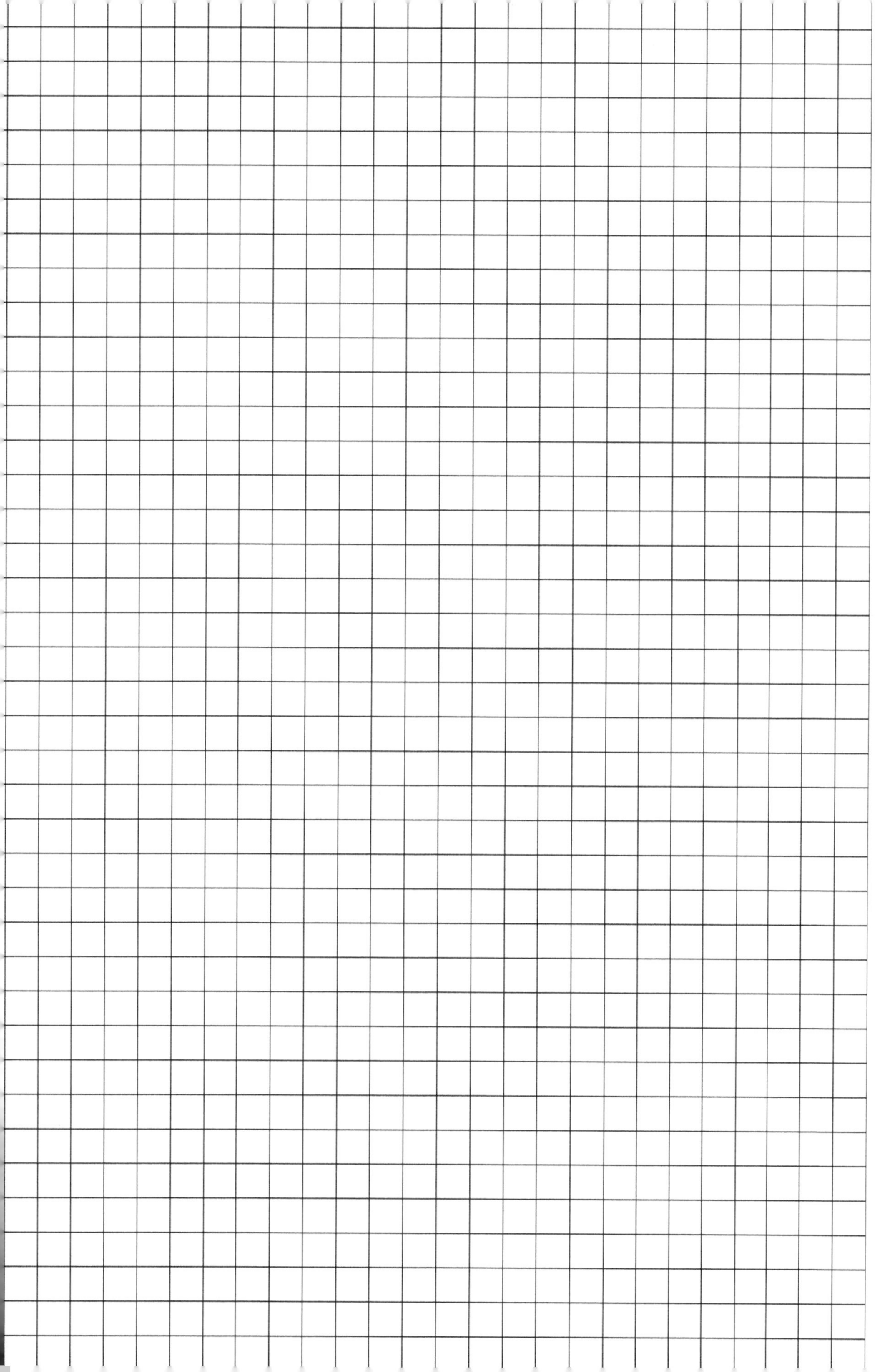

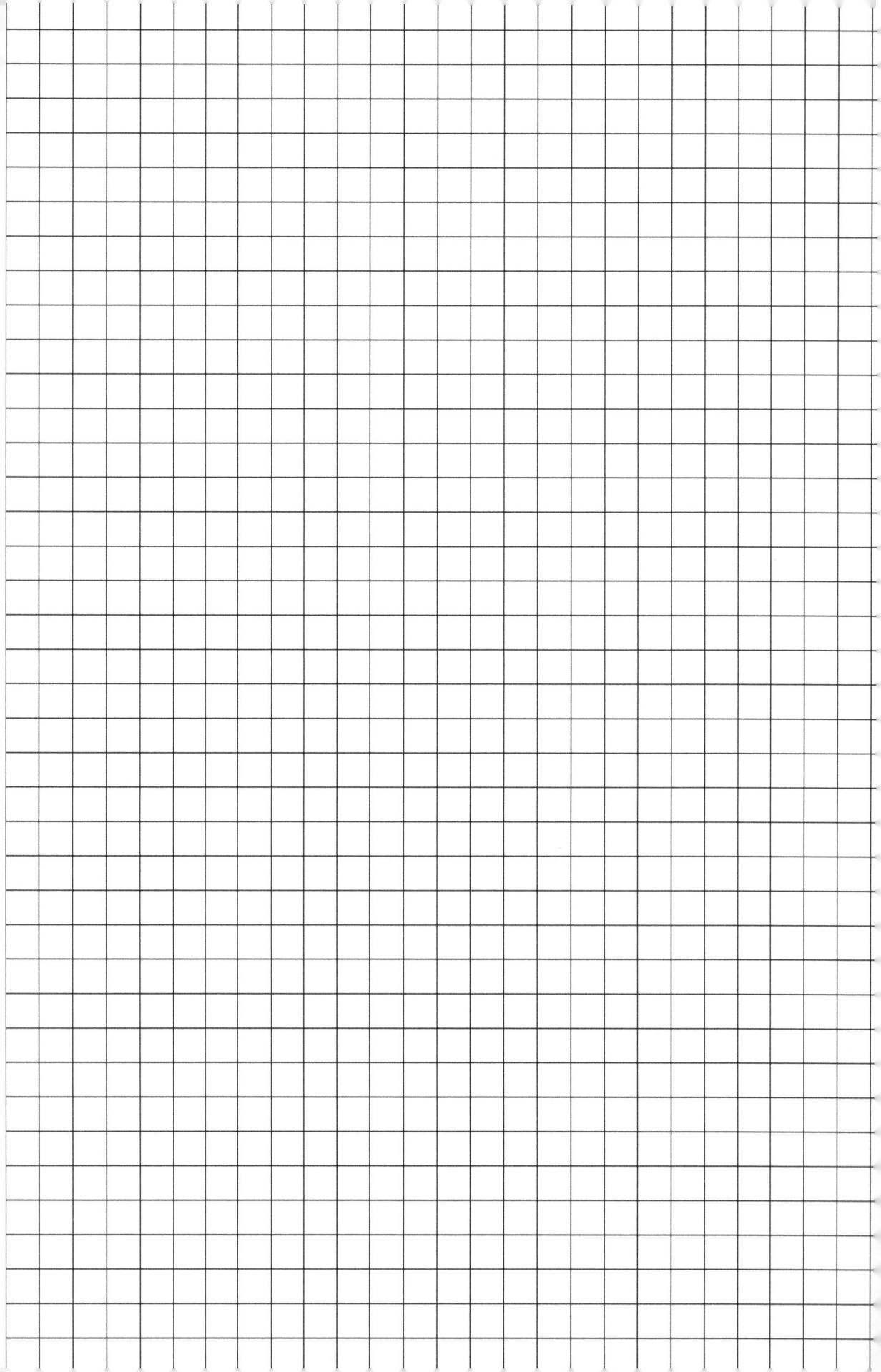

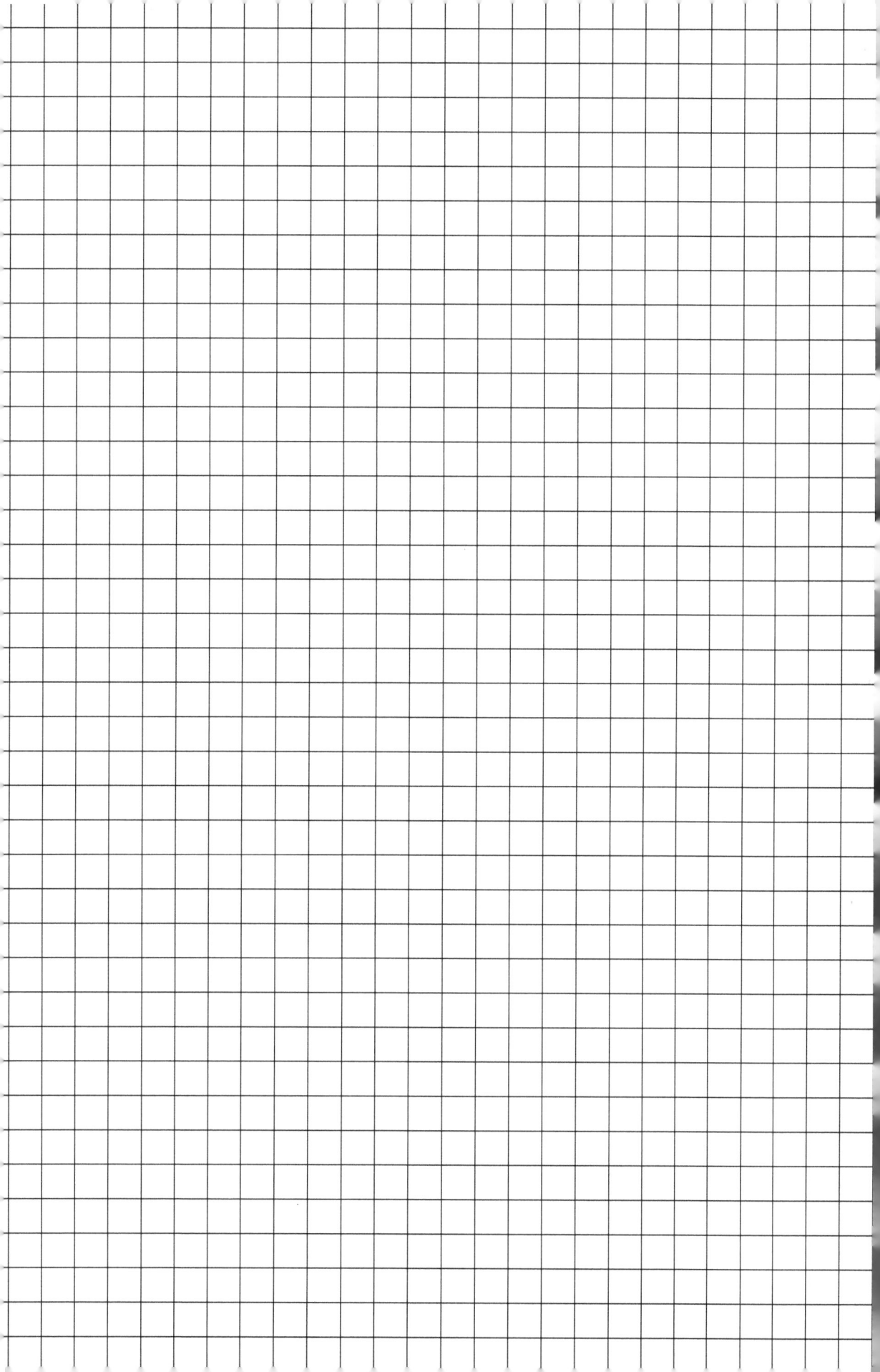

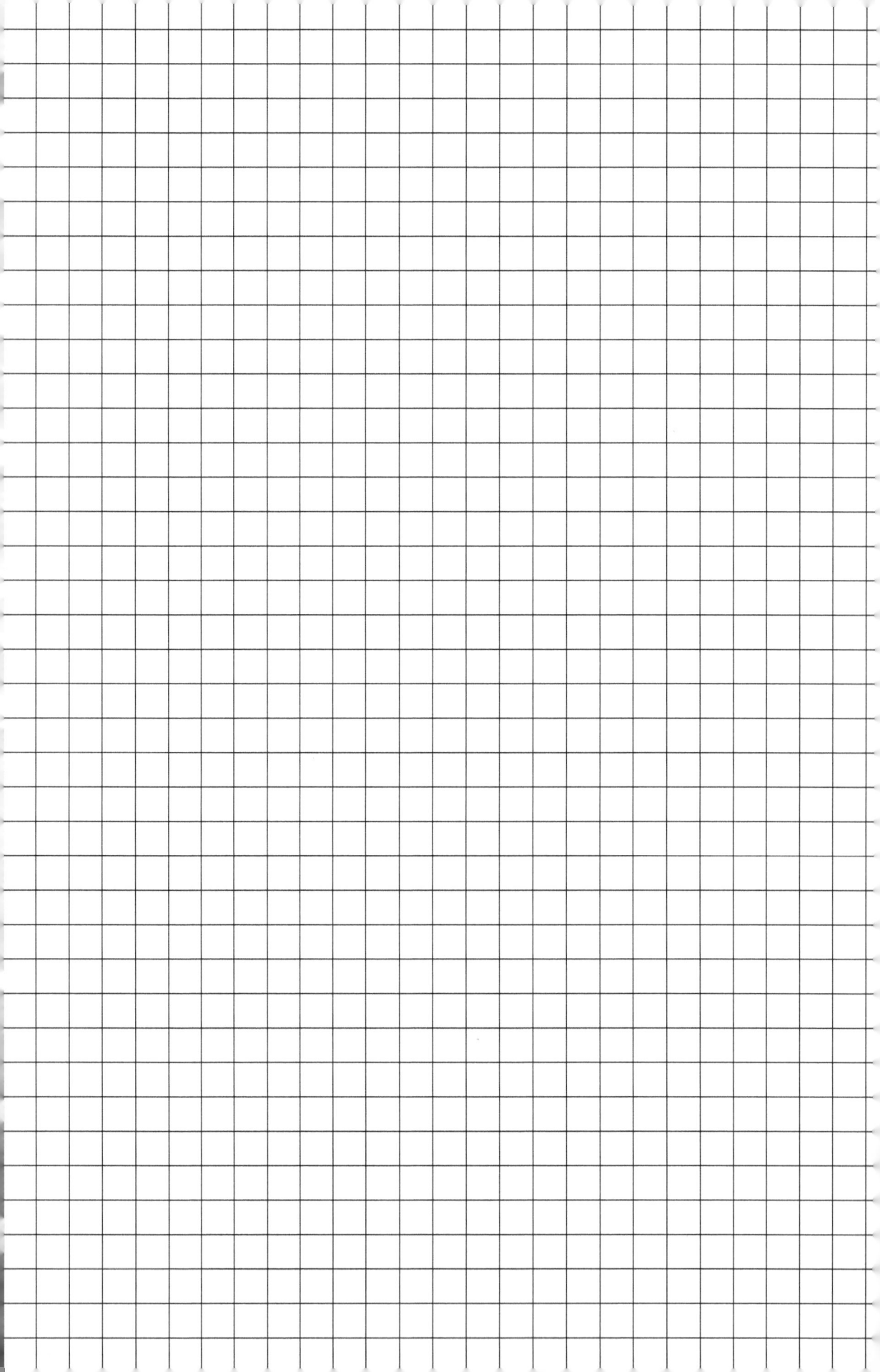

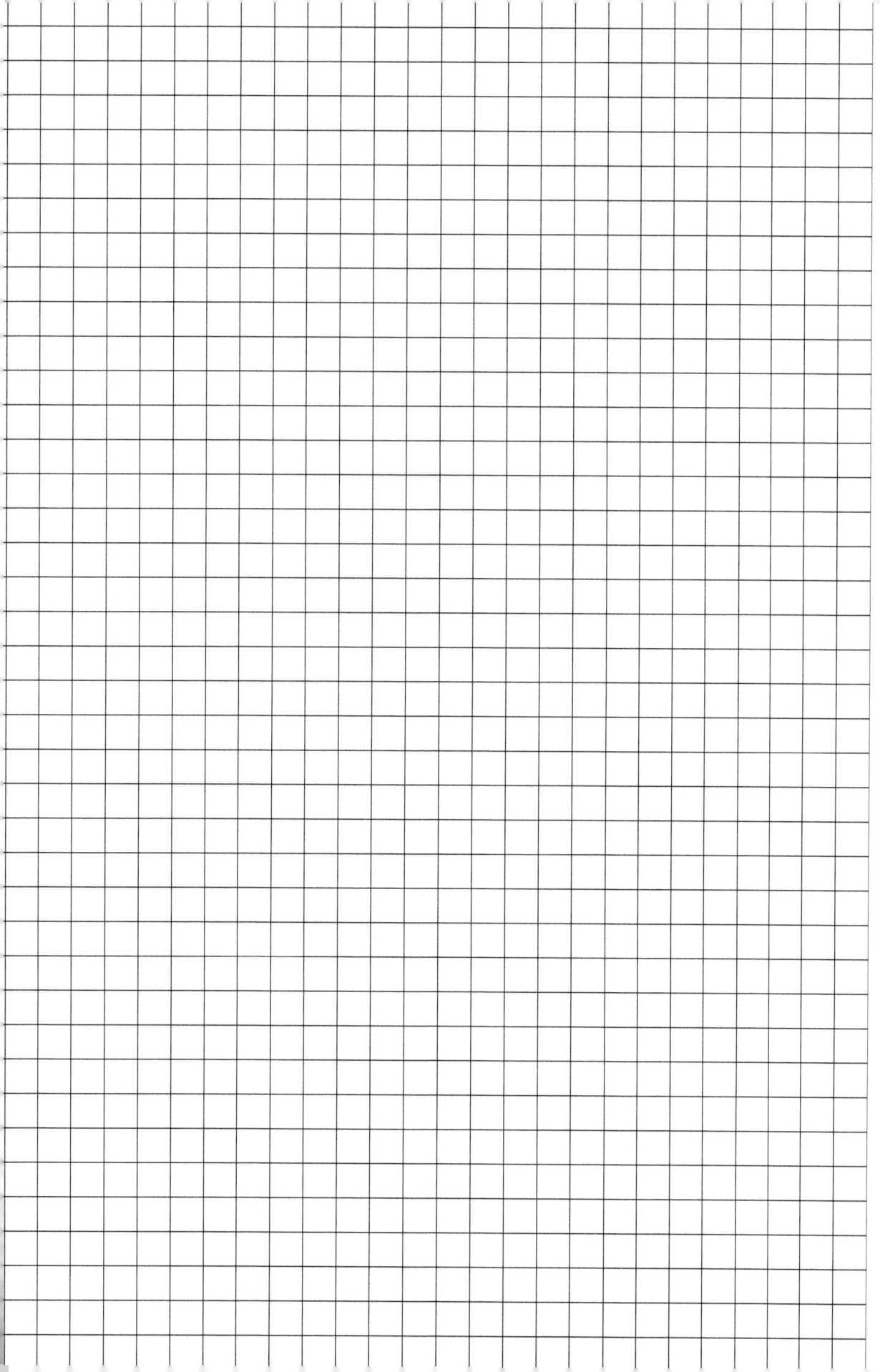

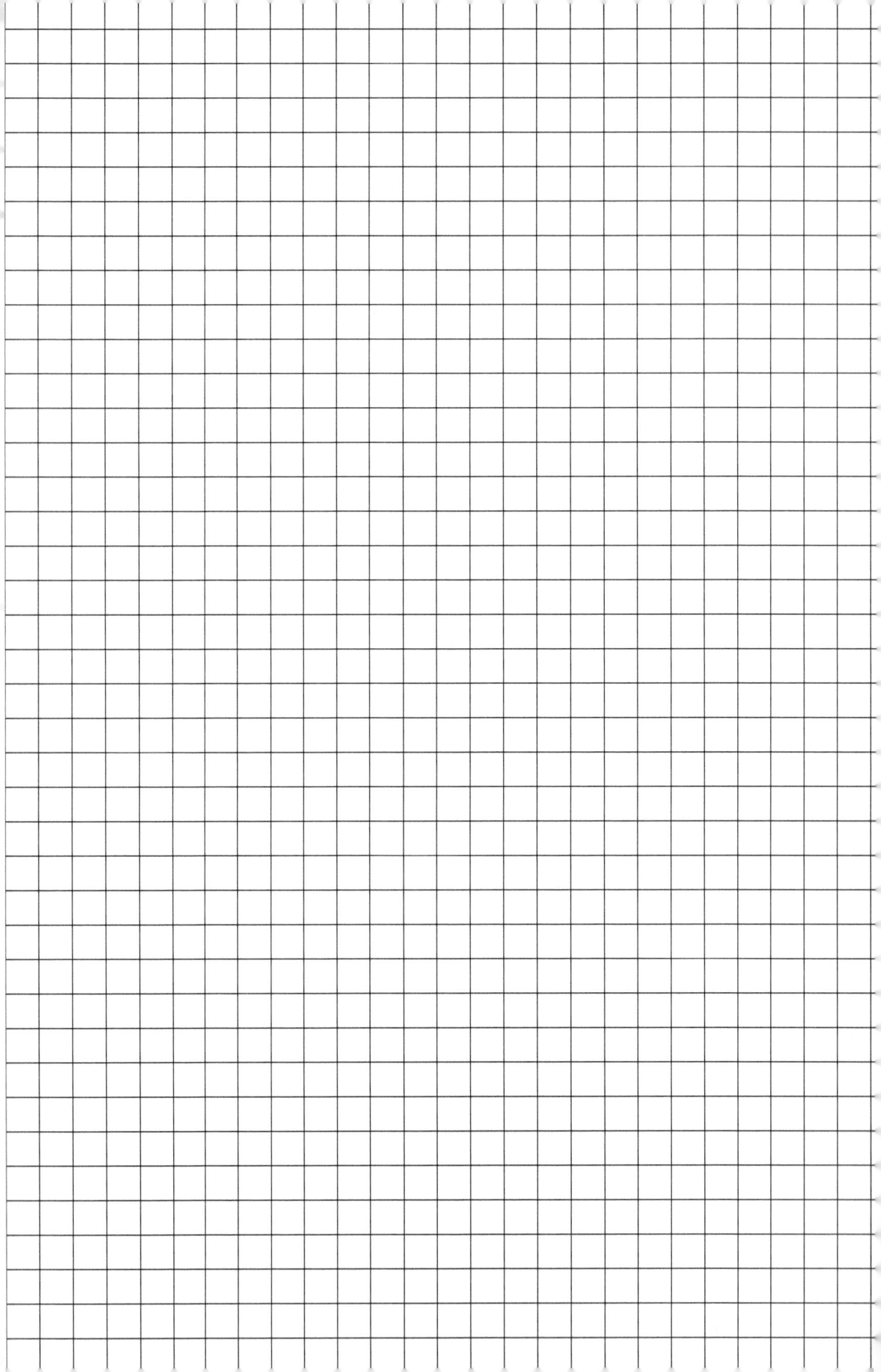

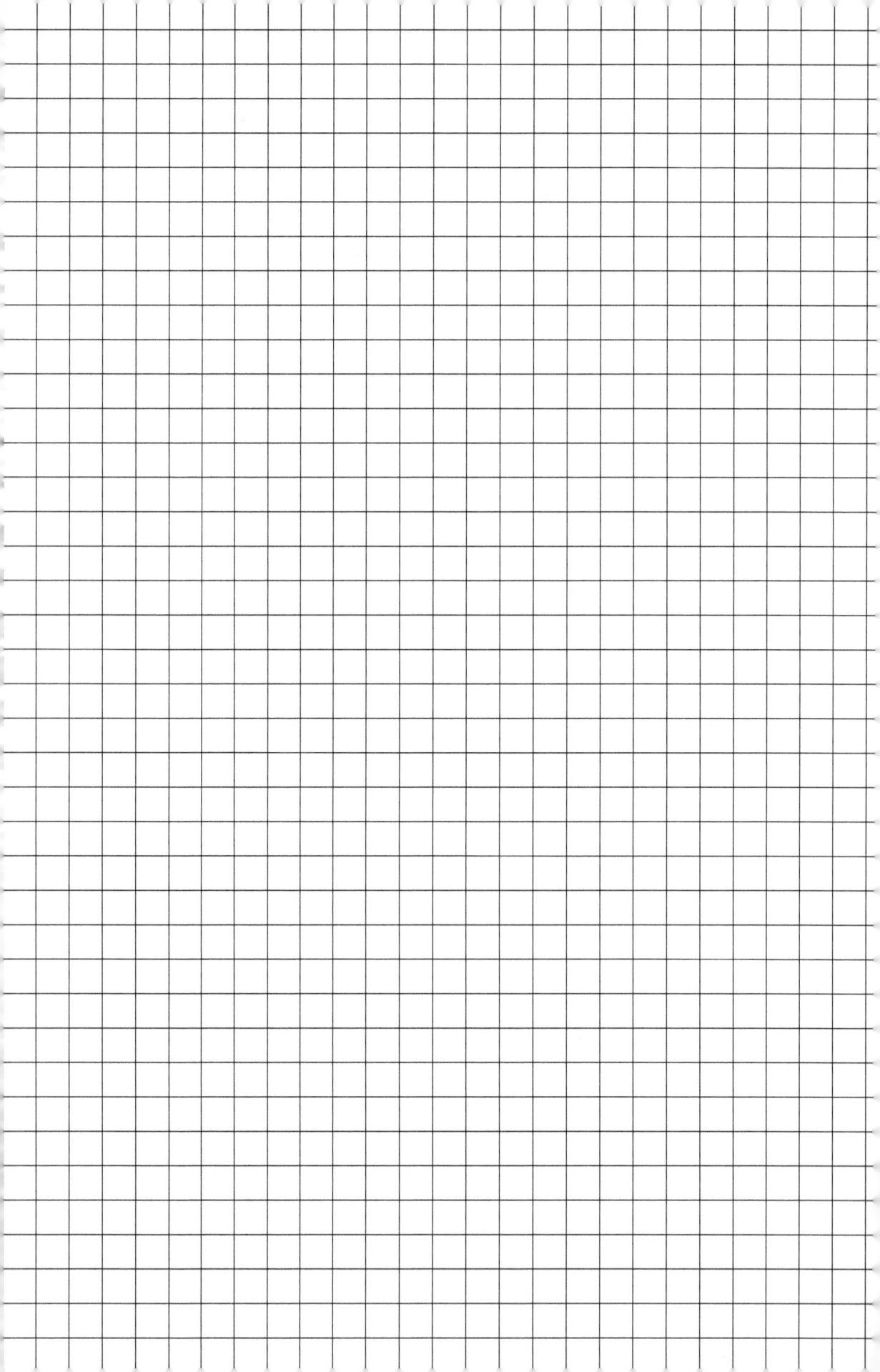

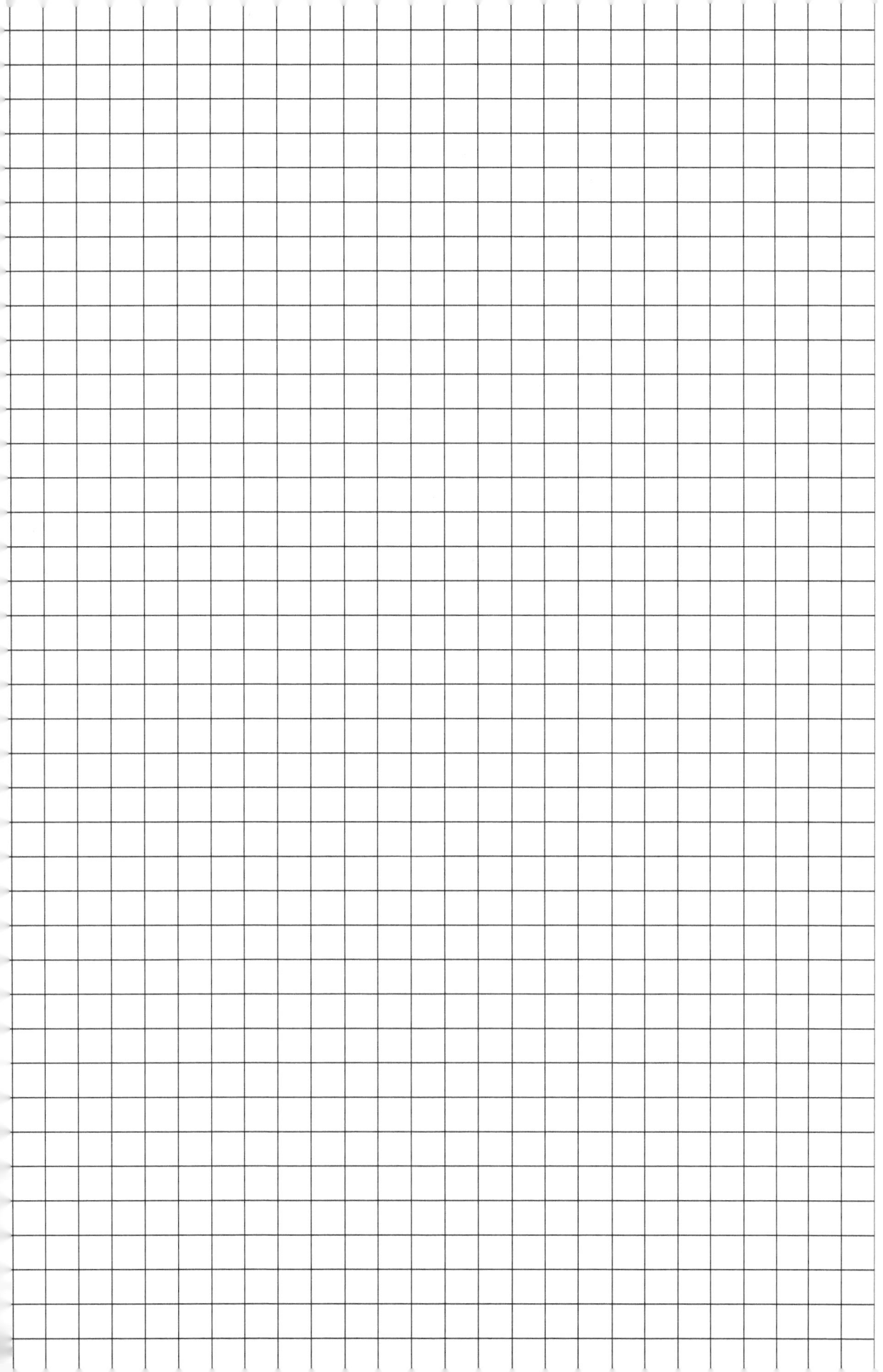

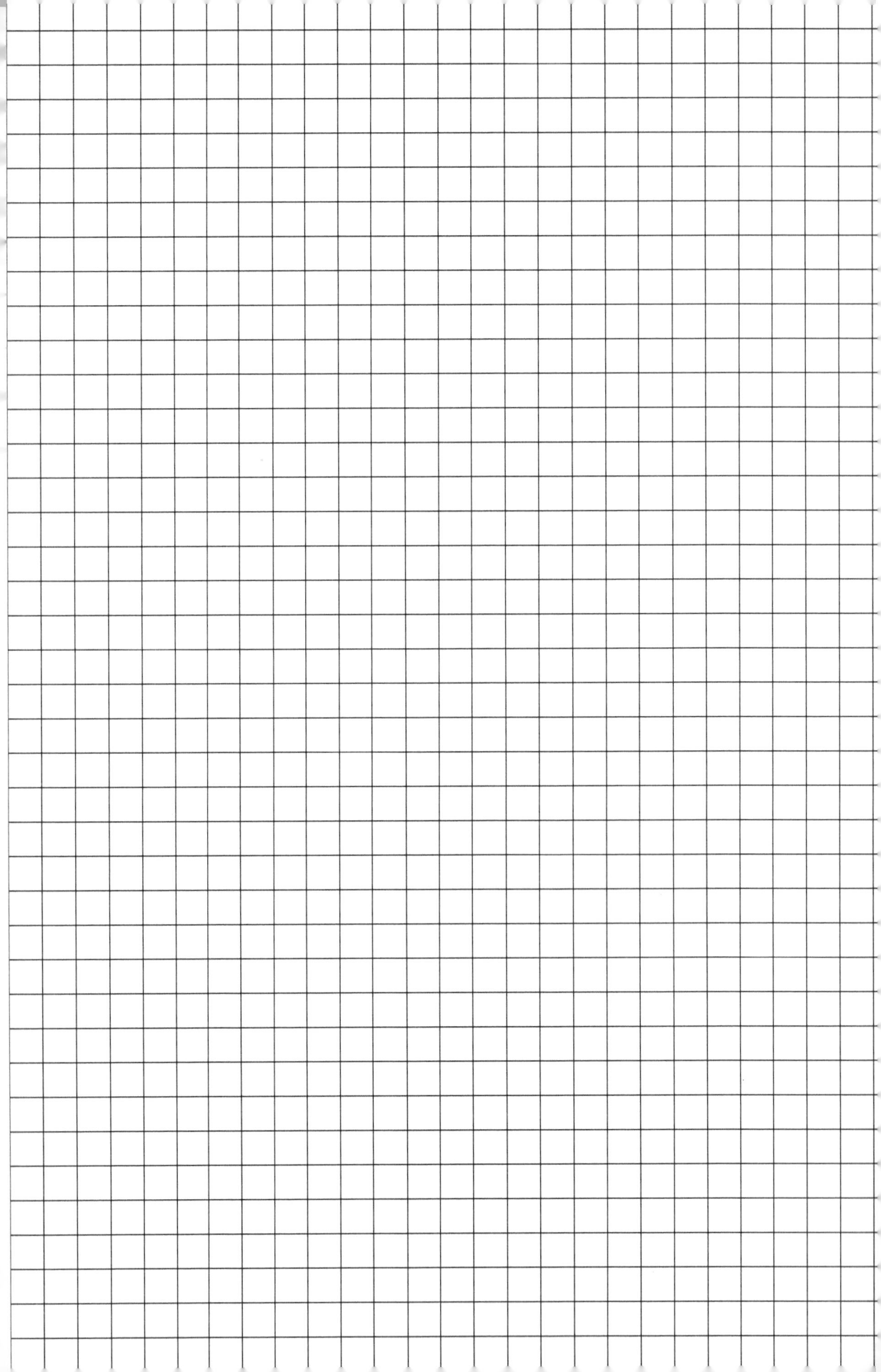

www.ingramcontent.com/pod-product-compliance
Lightning Source LLC
Chambersburg PA
CBHW052342210326

41597CB00037B/6226